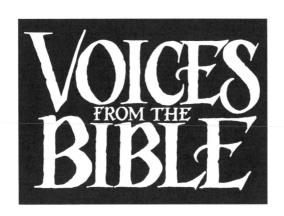

Dramatic Monologs in Worship

by
CALVIN S. METCALF

Photography by
KAREN CARDEN BIBBINS

MERIWETHER PUBLISHING LTD.
Colorado Springs, Colorado

Meriwether Publishing Ltd., Publisher
P.O. Box 7710
Colorado Springs, CO 80933

Editors: Karen C. Bibbins, Arthur L. Zapel
Typography: Sharon E. Garlock
Cover design: Tom Myers

© Copyright MCMXC Meriwether Publishing Ltd.
Printed in the United States of America
First Edition

Library of Congress Cataloging-in-Publication Data

Metcalf, Calvin S., 1934 —
    Voices from the Bible : dramatic monologs in worship / by Calvin
S. Metcalf. -- 1st ed.
      p.   cm.
   ISBN 0-916260-70-4
   1. Drama in Christian education.   2. Monologue sermons.
3. Sermons, American.   I. Title.
BV1534.4.M47   1990
246'.7--dc20
                                           90-53277
                                             CIP

ACKNOWLEDGEMENTS

Acknowledgement as well as appreciation are expressed to Karen Bibbins, who has been designer, photographer, typist and general consultant in the formation of this book. Without her expertise, it would never have made it to press. I am grateful also to the congregation of Central Baptist Church of Fountain City for giving me the inspiration to write and to perform biblical monologs as a serious contribution to Christian worship, and to a host of friends who have encouraged me to put this material in print.

Table of Contents

PREFACE

It is necessary to stir our imaginations from time to time. Dramatic monologs are an imaginative way to make the lives of our Bible heroes vivid and real. Perhaps they are a little more entertaining than ordinary pulpit fare, but performance must never be their sole purpose.

The people who laid Christianity's foundation have much to say to today's worshipers, and their messages are the most important aspect of this unique form of preaching. The costumes and make-up of these monologs are captivating, the delivery is dynamic, the content runs the gamut from wry humor to heartbreaking remorse, but woven through all of them is the Gospel thread. Each character reveals his personal contribution to, or participation in, God's plan for the redemption of humankind. Each one challenges twentieth-century believers to renew their commitments, to revitalize their dedication.

Voices from the Bible is a guide for observers who want to study and absorb words and personalities more deeply than they can during a single presentation. Why do certain characters emerge as they do? What were some historical influences on their lives? Were they really fearful, timid, belligerent, pompous . . . human?

It is a resource for clergy and other Christian speakers who seek a compelling alternative to routine sermons and speeches. Is achieving a biblical "look" expensive and complicated? Are props and staging necessary? When are movements and gestures appropriate?

Most important, however, this book is an expression of gratitude for the overwhelming response these monologs have evoked, for their humbling effectiveness and for the soul-nourishing worship they helped create. They can allow us to share with God's servants of ages past the burning desire to fulfill his reasons for our existence.

Maybe Joshua, himself, can speak best for Christendom's visiting forefathers: "You may be wondering why I have come here to recall for you these adventures from antiquity. I have come because I am a part of your tradition. You belong to my kind of faith. My people are your people, and my God is your God."

PREPARATION

Chapter One

WHY MONOLOGS?

Life is drama, and the lives of biblical characters are some of the most dramatic in all history. Most of us are accustomed to accepting the roles of these people somewhat blithely. Although we hear about them repeatedly throughout our lives, they usually remain distant and remote, in spite of the magnitude of their impact upon redemptive history. We need to experience the drama in their lives. If we spend more time getting to know them, getting in touch with their humanity, perhaps our studies will be more relevant and our worship more vivid.

Jonah, for instance, is known to us as a serio-comic prophet who was gulped down by a whale. Whether or not the "big fish" was a whale seems to be a favorite argument. But shouldn't our focus be on the man and his relationship with God? Jonah's response to both chastisement and success contain a multitude of insights into the personality who seeks to create its identity out of its religious position. How many of us are tempted to pout when God's activity threatens to diminish our reputation?

We need to wonder what went on in the minds and hearts of the people who helped shape our destinies. The Bible is not about fictitious characters who were created to convey contrived messages. Those names belonged to living, breathing, hurting, loving, sorrowing, rejoicing, suffering human beings. It is quite easy to lose sight of that.

Moses has been labeled one of the greatest leaders known to humankind. And so he was. But he was also one of the most reluctant, arguing with God at length about his appropriateness — or lack of it — for the task. In our backward glances, we tend to glimpse only at the brilliance and greatness of his career. How reassuring it is to temper our awe with his humanity! Also, how reassuring it is to expand our awe for God at his ability to work great things through people so much like we are!

The opportunity to identify with a person of God, to have a sense of being in close proximity to someone who was close to God, helps us feel we have been in God's presence. As these personalities unfold, we notice similarities to ourselves and realize we are not vastly different from them or each other. As they share their unique adventures so convincingly, we come to understand something of what God has in mind for us. Together, we see what God can do, what he has done and what he waits to do in us, and worship happens. Without worship, we lose fellowship with God and God's people.

Drama can be worship. Monologs must never become a "show" but must create the opportunity for genuine worship. The warmth of worship is vital to our spiritual glow. It keeps us close to the heat of heaven where the flame of God's love never flickers, and the light of his truth is an unquenchable fire. When we worship, we have a sense of reverence and praise. We need to ponder the things of God and to commit ourselves appropriately to him.

We need, also, to ponder the people of God. A dramatic monolog is a method of presenting truth from the imagined perspective of the character himself. This form of preaching is designed to let each one speak and come alive in our imaginations. Moods, feelings and interpretations are based on what Scripture reveals about a person. Subjects are chosen for monologs based on what they reveal about God and ourselves.

In worship, we find the burning desire to be God's person and to fulfill his reasons for our existence. Are those reasons the same as the ones for which he created the prophets and apostles of ages past?

Time is a factor, of course, and does not permit a look at all the intricate details of a character's life. A monolog will deal primarily with how external and internal pressures, personality type, lifestyle and religious orientation all combine to influence his behavior. It is good for us to observe expansive egos deflated in abject degradation, timidity turned into courage, humble submissiveness blessed and rewarded.

When we have to deal with boastful bigmouths, it is instructive to eavesdrop on how Jesus dealt with Simon Peter. When we've suffered the depression and frustration of losing a sure victory, it is encouraging to hear Elijah beg to die. When we find ourselves getting complacent about Bible study, it is inspiring to share John's eagerness to learn all he could about Jesus. In short, it always helps to feel we have met a kindred spirit.

Perhaps the spirits of Christendom's forebears cry out

most loudly for dramatic interpretation. The actual stories are important, but their familiarity creates a risk of our shallow response, our superficial application. Sometimes, the only dimension we allow their "stars" is the one portrayed in a specific story: Joseph and his coat of many colors; Judas, the betrayer; David, the giant killer. What motivated these people? What excited them? What defeated, frightened, propelled them? They are all deep, complex personalities whose messages to us far transcend the pigeonholes our stories sometimes capture them in.

Worship brings out the best that is in us, because it exposes us to the holiness of God. When real worship happens, we are never content to remain as we are. Our spiritual sights are raised, and we look beyond our selfish inclinations toward a new selflessness. Worship helps us revere that which is above and beyond us. It gives us a reason to be humble. It also gives us a reason to praise. The excitement of God's presence is always an occasion to sing and rejoice. Worship creates happiness in our grateful hearts, so we go forth joyfully to share with others what has transpired in our lives.

No life worthy of our study experienced an encounter with God and remained the same. We are helped to chart our own changes through worship experiences developed around people who met God and were transformed, who knew Jesus and became transformers. Monologs allow us to peep into the minds, hearts and souls of persons who have changed as we are changing . . . or should be.

Joseph, a spoiled young man who was the victim of his brothers' savage resentment, displays a rather unexpected capacity to forgive. He was able to see beyond his immediate troubles and discomforts to a divine purpose in all that happened to him. He did not whimper for the lost indulgences of his childhood and youth, but seized every opportunity to grow and serve. He was presented a made-to-order chance for revenge and struggled with its temptation. He chose instead to forgive, and not just forgive, but to help as one fortunate should help ones unfortunate, to love as family should love.

David speaks from his advancing years, a man who has lived an incredibly action-packed life, both physically and spiritually. "A man after God's own heart" is an apt description. He sought the heart of God no matter what his circumstances were. He rejoiced with his Lord at military and political successes. He talked with God about his failures and disappointments. He clung to God's forgiveness in the midst of immobilizing guilt and remorse. David the shepherd, David the king, David the sinner never ran away from, but toward, the God he often feared, sometimes dreaded, but upon whose love he knew he could depend.

Judas Iscariot represents the ultimate in misunderstanding. His refusal to change was his undoing. Whatever we choose to believe about the authenticity of his motives, his is potentially the story of every person. We are all vulnerable to the pressures of our times and the temptation to interpret everything in light of our favorite causes. We all share the tendency to misunderstand and to act tragically on that misunderstanding. Any one of us could, in the name of what we think is right, betray Jesus for a pittance of wealth, prestige or personal glory.

There are people in the Bible about whom little detail is given but who can contribute valuable perspectives on pivotal historical events. What Scripture does not say specifically about their character, personality and attitude, it often implies. One such man had a role in the dramatic birth of Jesus.

The person chosen to be the human masculine influence in Jesus' life had to have been steadfast, loyal, resolute and deeply honored to be selected to care for and nurture the Son of God. Joseph took some convincing about Mary's peculiar situation, but his desire to understand and his willingness to change allowed him a revelation of his own. He probably drew deeply from his Hebrew heritage to help validate his surrogate fatherhood. A humble and supportive man, he must have sensed the divine significance of being called, not to a heroic act or sacrificial servanthood, but called simply to love Jesus.

While he was not given a name, and might or might not have been a living person, the Prodigal Son illustrates a relationship Jesus was trying to define. This story is not a story about a wayward boy or even a loyal but jealous brother. It is a story about a loving father. The Prodigal Son was an innovative, adventuresome chap who yearned to explore life for himself. His discovery was disaster, but his independence got him a job, and his belief in his father's love lifted him from despair and sent him home. Convinced he had squandered his sonship, he fully intended to return as a servant. What awaited him is much more than a warm, tender ending to a nice story. It is the whole point.

One of the main functions of this type of preaching is to help us discover some of our own reasons for existing, as we observe in detail how others fulfilled their purposes. Joshua was a man who seems always to have been in preparation for the awesome responsibility that became his. Being a child of the exile was the first of his numerous credentials for leadership. He expressed his faith on many occasions and in various ways. His quiet understudy of Moses was another fiber being woven into his life-fabric. It is well to take Joshua as a model and look back on our past with a new perception of "so, that's why . . ."

There is no mystery about why Saul of Tarsus was caused to make a complete change of life and direction. This prolific writer and energetic missionary was one of the most influential personalities in the early years of Christianity. Any one of his exploits would yield itself to exciting dramatic interpretation, but perhaps his letter to the Corinthians distills for us the essence of what Paul was about. These words best express his feelings on Christian conflict and the heart of his approach to dissention in the church. It is not necessary to decide this letter was his most important contribution to the building of the Body of Christ, but it is certainly one worth bringing to our attention as memorably as possible.

In love, the Lord of life has given each of us a part in the drama of creation. In what ways are the talents and resources which God has placed at our disposal being used for his purposes? Selfish and indifferent people will never accept their parts in this drama. Their lines will go unlearned, and when the final curtain is drawn, there will be no applause from God for whom their lives were to have been a pleasure.

My endeavor is not to be an actor but to reproduce a bit of life that really was. The drama or worship does not end when a service ends. The real actors are the folks who portray their faith in praise and song and holy ordinances, then go out to portray their faith in the continuing drama of life.

Why, then, monologs? Because occasional visits by God's people of long ago can enhance our faith and our faithfulness today. Because we discover strengths to gird up and weaknesses to work on, as we listen to their triumphs and tragedies. Because Bible characters possessed personalities we can identify with, yieldedness we can learn from, commitment to which we can aspire. Because they were real, their reasons for living mirror our own, and their impact still reverberates across the centuries, as will our impact reverberate across centuries to come.

Chapter Two

CHARACTER DEVELOPMENT METHODS AND RESOURCES

What I look for first in a potential monolog character are the dramatic qualities of his life. Naturally, the more familiar personalities will have wider appeal and instant recognition, but they have become familiar because of the drama of their lives.

Sometimes the possibilities of someone's story will "simmer" in the back of my mind for weeks or even months. Other times, a special event or sermon series will spawn the development of a character. For instance, Jonah's struggle with God's assignment and the personal sacrifices involved in accepting it seemed to work in well with our foreign mission emphasis.

"John, the Beloved Disciple" was the final sermon in a series on the "I am . . . " sayings of Christ.

Annually during February, our congregation focuses on Christian love of God, church, family and self in a four-week celebration called "Love Month." Out of this event one year came the monolog on Paul, explaining the circumstances surrounding his famous love passage in his letter to the church at Corinth.

Rather than having something I want to say and seeking out a character who says it, I see a character who has something to say and seek to say it for him. There is an important difference. I spend a lot of time thinking about a person, empathizing with what he went through, trying to understand his responses to his circumstances. I construct conversations this person might have had with others. I do all I can to become that person, but I scrutinize my imagination very carefully so as not to violate Scripture. I let his character traits dictate my presentation. I must let him say what he is saying. A strong purpose of my own could result in a misinterpretation of his personality.

The Bible is the starting point for each character. It is the place of discovery as well as the beginning of research. After tracing all the Scripture passages available on a person, I turn to several different commentaries on those passages. I read biographies, biographical sketches, books on biblical times and customs, and sermon collections on biblical personalities. I study the political, financial and religious climate of a person's era and try to become familiar with the geography of his homeland or mission field.

An author can expect to gather considerably more information than will be used in the actual monolog. As fascinating and complex as most biblical characters are, a fifteen to twenty minute vignette will of necessity be a condensation of information. It is always better to have more material than is needed and condense it than not to research adequately and risk presenting a shallow message.

Joshua needed the most intensive research because material on him was difficult to find. He is perhaps the least known of the repertoire, having lived most of his life in Moses' shadow. He had to be brought out of hiding somewhat, and allowed to be the great man he was.

As might be expected, the least research went into the monolog on the Prodigal Son, since his character is rather narrowly defined in one story. Because there was little factual background on this character, more imagination went into designing his thought processes and actions.

The "what if" factor is frequently involved in choosing and developing personalities. What if Judas wasn't really a murderous traitor? What if we could be privy to Joseph's anguish as he listened to his beloved Mary's incredible news? What if Paul could share his concern for a faltering congregation with us?

Since it is the author's responsibility to accurately define a character in a valid spiritual and historical context, the process is more observation than creation. While a character may be chosen for certain unique personal attributes, what must emerge to make him relevant are his universally human traits.

Joseph of Nazareth is a somewhat neglected character of the Christmas story. I wanted to bring him out of obscurity and show him to be the man of faith he must have been. He was willing to forsake his doubts and misgivings about Mary's situation and accept the almost unbelievable truth. He exhibited obedience, patience, caring and creativity in his guardianship of first the mother of our Lord and then our Lord himself.

David is one of the strongest personalities in the entire Bible. His lifestyles led him from peaceful sheep pastures to exile as a wilderness warrior; from peasanthood to a king's wealth; from the ecstasies of military and political triumph to personal tragedy and family chaos. He experienced deep and lingering sadness and was definitely a broken man but never a defeated one.

Elijah, perhaps the most dramatic of all the prophets, was a walking sermon with many topics. His was a volatile, exciting ministry highlighted by miracles but punctuated with misery. He was emotionally erratic, unable to deal objectively with the aftermath of Jehovah's manifestation on Mt. Carmel. He possessed a capacity for great rage, yet he dealt kindly and gently with widows. Everything we know about Elijah makes his personality ideal for dramatic interpretation.

As has been mentioned before, "John, the Beloved Disciple" was developed as the final sermon in a series based on the "I am . . ." sayings of Jesus. John's account is different from the synoptic gospels in that it doesn't present Jesus' life in chronological order. John spoke to the Greek-thinking world of his day and brought a freshness, a sense of personal dedication to his reporting. He seemed to have enjoyed a unique closeness to Jesus which distinctly influenced his narrative.

Jonah's story is essentially a missionary story. Still, the quick glance at him which the Scriptures allow us reveals a complex man ruled by prejudice but capable of repentance, bigoted but really wanting to please God. By his preconceived notions of how God should behave, he kept setting himself up for deep disappointment. The "unfinished book" of Jonah leaves us wondering about the rest of his career as a prophet. Did he ultimately acquire a genuine attitude of yieldedness as this monolog suggests, or did he continue to struggle against the universality of the love he was to proclaim?

Joseph, the son of Jacob, is an example of a monolog in which the message comes first and the personality is of secondary importance. He summed up his philosophy of life in one profound statement to his brothers: "While you meant it for bad, God meant it for good." Perhaps it was Joseph's naturally gracious spirit that allowed God's grace to dominate every potentially disastrous situation in which he found himself. He was truly a survivor and one who survived without malice or bitterness.

Joshua is another character (like Mary's Joseph) who seemed to cry out to us from relative obscurity. He occupied a pivotal position in the history of mankind, and his voice is well worth hearing. He was a man right for his times. He met the challenges of land acquisition and division with stern military discipline and deep loyalty to his God and his people.

Judas Iscariot, unique among the disciples, is probably the most misunderstood and maligned figure in the New Testament. His mystique and his nature need to be interpreted for us to understand the dimensions of life the gospel addresses. The kinds of things Judas represents are the kinds of things the gospel deals with: disappointment that leads to faithlessness; disillusionment that dissolves loyalty; restlessness that replaces grace with greed; dissatisfaction that forsakes the way of the cross.

One of the most dramatic personalities of the Old Testament, Moses needs to be seen and heard today. In him, we find an obedient servant-leader whose personal faith inspired the faith of his followers. He was a meek yet mighty instrument of God who did not rely on himself but on the power and promises of his Jehovah.

The apostle Paul is to the New Testament what Moses is to the Old Testament — a powerful personality who needs visibility and a forum. This particular monolog reveals Paul's compassionate nature and his commitment to the heart of the gospel which is agape love. He communicates the importance of love with intensity, as he pours out his impassioned, agonizing concern for a struggling church.

The story of the Prodigal Son is our Lord's most famous parable. It is personally intriguing to visit with a cocky young man who made a dramatic about-face from arrogant self-centeredness to repentant humility. While the wandering son may represent those of us who have to hit bottom before we can look upward, his story isn't really about the consequences of his behavior. Every step of his journey away and every step of it toward home points to the waiting, loving father.

Simon Peter, the most vocal of the disciples, offers us another opportunity to watch human nature in transition. From boisterous and braggadocious, he became mellow and submissive. His spiritual over-confidence caused his greatest mistake and his greatest heartache, but recovery from them created one of the greatest witnesses Christendom has ever known.

Chapter Three

COSTUMES, MAKE-UP TIPS, AND PROPS

Costumes

A character's visual personality contributes greatly to how the audience feels about him and responds to what he has to say. As much effort should go into researching a character's dress as goes into exploring his life and times.

Fabric color and design contribute to his impact and effectiveness. Judas, for instance, would probably have been a conservative, if not a downright frugal, dresser. Therefore, flamboyance and brilliant colors would not provide a believable representation of him as a financial fanatic.

On the other hand, David, portrayed in his later years, is expected to be majestic, regal, opulent. He should wear the rich colors of royalty with lavish-looking braid, trims and jewels. Gold-colored rickrack of all sizes, packaged gold decorations, drapery cord, etc., can be used to adorn a king's raiment.

Joseph, Jacob's son, is renowned for his indulgent father's gift of a "coat of many colors." Vividly and brightly multicolored striped fabric comes to mind for his famous garment.

In contrast, the Prodigal Son is expected to be dirty, threadbare and disheveled. He should wear clothes with the look of extreme deprivation and appear to have spent some time in a pigpen.

Children's Bible storybooks are an excellent source for authentic, uncomplicated pictures. Other children's Bible study resource materials such as bulletin board pictures, filmstrips and Sunday school papers also contain usable artist's impressions.

More sophisticated information is available from commentaries, Bible dictionaries and encyclopedias. Knowing what types of fabric were used in ancient times is helpful in locating the weight or finish which would most closely resemble the dress of the day. Movies and television shows provide still another source for costuming and allow the viewer to pay particular attention to how a moving character looks in a certain type of garment and how the garment hangs or flows or drapes or bulges during certain activity. It is helpful to try on a prototype of a planned costume and practice the movement and gestures the character will make.

The comfort of the performer is a valuable consideration as costumes are being designed. If a sleeveless robe threatens to fall off one shoulder or if a turban dips, he cannot relax and proceed confidently. A costume should not restrict movement or gestures. If shoes or sandals are worn, they should fit comfortably and securely. When an item of the costume is directly involved in the monolog (Elijah's mantle, Moses' shoes, the Prodigal's robe, Judas' purse), its original design or an adaptation should allow for worry-free ease of handling.

Lightweight fabrics are best if a costume contains multiple layers. Dramatic presentations are physically demanding. Add to this exertion spotlights, a crowded room or airless stage area, and maintaining a bearable temperature becomes a serious problem.

All the major sewing pattern companies offer well-designed patterns for biblical era costumes. Most will include under and outer garments, robes and head covers. Some even offer instructions on the assembly of "armor," tunics, leggings, shields and other military accouterments.

Besides commercial patterns, there are several options for a creative costume designer. The sixties and early seventies provided the caftan craze, and patterns for such long, large, flowing clothes, make good starting places for biblical attire. A floor-length caftan with long sleeves would make an appropriate king's robe. The same pattern with shorter sleeves and higher hemline would make an excellent overskirt or slave's garment. A hooded caftan might clothe a shepherd or a beggar.

Appropriately colored bathrobes with the sleeves cut out can serve in certain circumstances. Stay alert for fabric possibilities in places other than a piece goods store. Sheets, spreads or curtains (old or new) might provide just the right appearance.

Since most characters will be viewed from a distance, many unexpected items create functional illusions. Brown or tan leg warmers wrapped with crisscrossed leather thongs look to the audience like high-topped laced boots or sandals. Gold or silver belting is rigid and shiny and is excellent for arm bands, crowns and bracelets.

Headbands can be purchased ready-made. They also can be elastic covered with the same fabric as the costume or coordinated colors twisted or braided.

Authenticity is always a goal to pursue in creating a Bible character's "look." Still, there are many inexpensive, easy to obtain materials a costume designer can use to bring the chosen personality to life.

Make-up Tips

The amateur presenter of monologs need not invest heavily in theatrical make-up to change his appearance adequately. An item or two from theater suppliers, the rest from a drugstore cosmetic counter and a few tips from the pros will transform anyone into the character of his choice.

The key word in making up for the stage is "excess." Overdo everything. Distance from the viewers, special effects or inadequate lighting, the absence of a backdrop or scenery all combine to make a monolog character's face difficult to see. Often, facial expressions are critical for a successful dramatic portrayal.

Start with a foundation to darken face and neck. Since my Anglo-Saxon whiteness doesn't always seem appropriate for a swarthy Jew, I often use leg make-up on my feet, ankles or legs, hands and forearms. Charcoal gray or deep blue eye shadow on upper and lower lids deepens the eye sockets and makes eyes more visible. Apply black, brown or gray eyebrow pencil to darken and enlarge eyebrows and deepen wrinkles in the forehead, around the mouth and at eye corners. Eyebrow pencils also serve well to color areas where a wig or an applied beard does not cover completely.

To make an area recede, darken it. To make it stand out or appear large, lighten or highlight it.

Lightly brush cheekbones and forehead just above brows with blush. This not only adds color, it also helps draw viewers' attention to the eyes.

The clean-shaven dramatist will need a beard for practically every male biblical monolog subject. Here is where a theatrical supply store is helpful. A simple and inexpensive beard is made of crepe hair, which is a braid or string of fibers to be pulled apart, pressed, custom trimmed and shaped. (Moses' and Elijah's beard are made of hair cut from the long, silver wig they wear.) This is applied to a base of nylon netting.

Always build a beard on your face. Cut the nylon into the basic shape of your jaw and chin lines. Apply latex to your face and press the nylon into it. Next, arrange the beard on the net-and-latex base, being careful to cover evenly. Remove the whole beard and allow to dry at least a couple of hours, preferably overnight. Use spirit gum for repeatedly attaching a finished beard.

After a beard is pulled off, spirit gum remover is the best product for quick removal of residue. Denatured alcohol or other gentle solvents will also clean the face with minimal discomfort to the skin. Eye make-up, eyebrow pencil and foundation come off best with a cleansing cream or petroleum jelly.

A small collection of wigs will serve several monolog characters. A dark brown short style is probably the most versatile wig in my collection. A longer gray one works well for the older characters, and Moses and Elijah share a full, flowing silver one.

Here again, the costumer's creativity helps keep down costs and maintain authenticity. If a wig's shape or cut is not quite right for the look you have in mind, try putting it on backward.

Props

Since the majority of my monolog presentations are in church sanctuaries, I have kept the need for props to a minimum. Only one of these monologs calls for furniture. Most of the props are integral parts of their costumes.

Elijah's mantle is made of long, shaggy fake fur which passably resembles goat hair. It has elastic straps which hold it securely over the shoulders and under the arms. When it is time for it to fall, a discreet tug will slip the straps over the shoulders and allow it to slide off.

Since Joshua and Moses both tread holy ground and are commanded to take off their shoes, easily removable sandals are the most authentic looking for these characters.

The same sandals will work for the Prodigal Son, who has no shoes to take off, but puts some on toward the end of his monolog. He also needs a large, straight, colorful robe to slip into and a large gold-colored ring to place on his finger.

Judas Iscariot's main prop is an old, worn leather purse or pouch filled with coins. Ideally, the contents should jingle with most of his movements throughout his monolog. On several occasions, he gestures with the pouch, then finally throws it angrily to the floor. Obviously, it must have a zipper or some other dependable closure to keep its contents from scattering.

In addition to easy on-and-off shoes, Moses needs a shepherd's crook or a long pole.

Paul is the only character whose monolog calls for props other than costume elements. This one needs a small table and chair or short wooden stool. It could be a child's table or a small writing desk. The furniture pieces should be wood and look old. Paul doesn't actually sit at the desk and write, but it needs to look like he could have. A deckle-edged or torn piece of parchment (bought at an artist's supply store) is on the desk. The portion of the letter he reads to his listeners could be written directly on the parchment. A genuine quill perched in a desk-top pen holder would be a nice touch for the desk. A plumed pen will do nicely if the plastic part is not too obvious to viewers.

Costumes. Make-up. Props. All instruments of the imagination to help bring to our lives a life lived centuries ago. Perhaps the words could stand alone. Perhaps these theatrical trappings are not really necessary. But the costuming and other efforts toward authentic recreation of who these people were and how they probably looked contribute greatly to my ability to "get into" a character. If I cannot submerge my own personality into the spirit and personality I am portraying, how convincing can he be? If I cannot surrender who I am to who he was, just for the moment, what of spiritual substance will he have to say to us?

I know, too, that delivery of monologs in costume helps transport viewers to another time, another place. Their involvement in the worship experience is enhanced because they are challenged to do more than sit and listen. They are caused to remember events surrounding a certain adventure. They are invited to learn from the successes and failures of influential people. They are encouraged to believe these people were real and contributed generously to the rich Christian heritage we share.

The greatest result I can hope for from the presentation of a monolog is that hearts will be turned toward the God of yesterday and today. The greatest compliment I hear is, "I completely forgot it was you."

PRESENTATION

Joseph

A CARPENTER'S DREAM
Matthew 1:18-25

Sometimes, it helps to take a careful look at what those closest to an event might have been thinking and feeling. It is a source of encouragement to stop and realize that our Christmas characters were real live people. No other personality in that manger scene has as awkward an assignment as Joseph. He was husband, but not father. He was definitely involved, but very much in the background of that holy happening. What went on in the mind and heart of the man called in a special way to history's most unusual birth? What qualities did he possess which enabled him to serve such a vital role with so little attention? Joseph represents ordinary people who may never make the headlines, but who, nonetheless, are essential to the progress of God's Kingdom.

Props: None needed
Delivery time: 15-20 minutes

(JOSEPH speaks heartily and directly to audience.)
Congratulations! You are a privileged people to be able to celebrate the birth of Jesus with such lavish attention toward one another. You are to be commended for your benevolent spirit toward those in need and your generous gifts for world missions.

You and your kind have come a long way from that simple stable setting of years ago. *(Thoughtfully)* **Who would have believed the miracle of a manger would have affected the course of human history in such a way that today the birth of Jesus is the world's most celebrated event?**

(With slight amusement) **I see some of you looking a bit puzzled at me. I assume you want to know who I am. I am Joseph, the husband of Mary, who is the mother of the baby, Jesus, you so often sing about. It's quite possible you have given little thought to my role in the Christmas**

story. After all, I was pretty much in the background of that holy event.

(*Matter-of-fact*) Oh, yes, I am in the pictures. You've seen the picture of me leading a donkey laden with my pregnant wife, as we made our way toward Bethlehem. You've seen the picture of me pleading at the innkeeper's door for a room. You've placed me in your Nativity scenes beside Mary, with shepherds, sheep and cattle mingling around the manger child. Oh, yes, I'm in the pictures.

Perhaps you have always thought I had an insignificant place in the birth of Jesus, and in many ways you are right. But I never thought so ... once I understood. (*Emphatically*) I felt I was the most privileged of all men to be the guardian of the Christ child. What honor God had bestowed upon me! What trust, to give *me* the care of his Son! Therefore, let me tell you the Christmas story from my perspective.

(*Sadly, regretfully*) At first, I did not understand. When Mary came telling me she was expecting a child, I thought my heart would break. Why would she do this to me? After all, we were engaged to be married. Then, when she told me she had conceived by the Holy Spirit, confusion was added to my grief.

I had heard many excuses before, but this one was rare indeed! Was Mary trying to tell me God approved of her promiscuous ways? How could God possibly condone such behavior?

Surely, something had happened to Mary. She was the last woman in the world I would suspect of such an indiscretion. Of all the people I knew, Mary was undoubtedly the most devout. At first, I became angry because I thought someone had taken advantage of her, and she was trying to protect him.

Although grief and pain and frustration were my constant companions, I knew something had to be done.

After all, when her pregnancy became generally known, my own good name would be threatened. I knew I had to put Mary away. I had to break our engagement, but I loved her. *(With much feeling)* Oh, how I loved her!

(Still with regret) I could not bring myself to report her to the authorities. I knew they would treat her without mercy. The law was so severe on matters like that. I could not have lived with myself had I allowed the law to punish my dear, dear Mary. I decided to make it a private matter. But, oh, it was breaking my heart to tell Mary it was all over!

Perhaps I will wait another day before I tell her our marriage is off, I thought. In the meantime, I spent long hours in prayer asking God if I was doing the right thing and doing it the right way. I fell asleep at my prayers, and it was in my sleep that God opened the eyes of my spirit.

(With wonder) The angel of the Lord appeared to me in a dream and told me not to fear taking Mary as my wife. He also assured me her pregnancy was an act of the Holy Spirit. Even in my dream it must have been apparent that I needed more convincing.

In my vision, the angel seemed to take me back through time. Suddenly, I was looking in on Abraham, and God was saying to him, "I will bless you and make your seed as sand of the sea. I will establish with you and your descendants an everlasting covenant, and in you all the families of the earth shall be blessed."

I saw all the patriarchs when God was renewing his covenant with his people through them. I saw Joseph in Egypt request that his bones be carried back to the Land of Promise, as a gesture of hope which he had for Israel.

I was carried in my dream to the top of Mt. Nebo, where I looked with Moses at the Land of Promise. I heard him challenge Joshua and all Israel to be strong and of great courage, because God had many plans for his people. The angel allowed me to see the judges of Israel, as they led the people in their struggling determination to keep the land God had given them. Never before had I understood the sacrifices of my forefathers. Surely, God had a mighty plan.

Then, I found myself in Jerusalem. It was a time of celebration. David was bringing the Ark of the Covenant to rest in the Holy City. It was to be the capital of God's people filled with all his hopes and dreams. Later, I was to see Solomon display the Temple as a showpiece for God to all the world. Here again, God's covenant was reviewed, and a commitment from the people was renewed.

Once more, my vision took me through the years. I was looking over Isaiah's shoulder as he wrote, "The people who walk in darkness have seen a great light. To those who live in a dark land, on them the light will shine. For unto us a child is born; unto us a Son is given. And the government shall be upon his shoulders. And his name shall be called Wonderful Counselor, the Mighty God, the Everlasting Father, the Prince of Peace, and of the increase of his government there shall be no end."

The days of Isaiah were dark and dismal. I sensed his power to dream God's dream, as he looked down the corridor of time toward the majestic Messiah.

I was carried to the countryside where Micah lived with people crushed by the power of an unfair government. Under the inspiration of God, he was writing of a time when a true king would come. This is what I saw him write: "But thou, Bethlehem Ephratah, though thou be little among the thousands of Judah, yet out of thee shall he come forth unto me that is to be the ruler in Israel. Whose goings forth have been from of old, from everlasting."

The place will be Bethlehem. The person will be Messiah.

(With growing excitement) As my dream ended, the angel reminded me of Isaiah's Messianic sign: "Behold, a virgin shall conceive and bring forth a Son, and they shall call his name Immanuel, which means 'God with us.'" The angel also told me that Isaiah's virgin was none other than my own dear Mary.

As I was waking, it seemed as though I kept hearing people say, "Don't be afraid, Joseph." It seemed as though Abraham and all the patriarchs were saying it, Moses and all the judges, David and all the godly kings, Isaiah, Micah and all the prophets. In fact, all the spiritual personalities of my Hebrew heritage were encouraging me to take Mary and not to be afraid, because she was to be an important person in holy history.

The angel insisted I marry Mary, because the Son in her womb was of God. Mary had not been unfaithful to me. She had been faithful to God. It would be my duty as her husband to name the God-child Jesus, for he would save his people from their sins.

(Excitedly) When I awoke, things began to clear up. If God's Son were going to be born into this world, then only the purest virgin could bear that seed. By her unquestionable purity, the miracle of her godly conception would be validated. And to think, my own dear Mary was chosen by God for this awesome assignment! *(Slightly facetiously)* Apparently, I had pretty good taste in women.

I could hardly wait to tell Mary about my dream! I was so ashamed of myself for doubting her integrity. *(With amazement)* Isn't it wonderfully strange how God works? He turned what I thought was a questionable romance into a divine mission. He gave me more love for Mary than I ever imagined was possible! Not only was I going to be the husband of my dear, dear Mary, I was going to be the custodian of God's dear Son.

(With great excitement) We began immediately to make plans for our wedding. It was as though God himself performed the ceremony and the angels in heaven were our attendants. But marriage was not the most important item on the agenda of our lives at that time. We had to care for the child to be born and the Son which was to be given.

Near the time Mary was to be delivered of her child, we had to go to Bethlehem to participate in the census of Caesar Augustus. To some, it may have seemed like a cruel thing for Mary to make the trip to Bethlehem in her condition. It's possible I could have gotten permission for her to stay in Nazareth, but there had been too much talk in town. I wanted Mary by my side. I wanted to protect her myself.

I wanted to care for her in that tender hour of childbirth. It didn't bother me that her child might be born in Bethlehem. In fact, I rather expected it. Deep within me, I kept hearing Micah say, "But thou, Bethlehem Ephratah, though thou be little among the thousands of Judah, out of thee shall come a ruler."

As we suspected, the long trip prompted her labor and there we were in crowded Bethlehem, desperately needing a room. The only thing we could get was the innkeeper's stable. At best, it was mere protection from the cold night air. We had little time, however, to worry about the crude surroundings. We had to do the best we could with what we had, for in a short time after we arrived, Mary delivered her Son.

(Dreamily, with a sense of wonder) It was then our simple stable was changed into a palace! The straw glistened like gold, as a special star shone from above. The sky burst forth with brilliance, and all heaven seemed

to celebrate the birth of Mary's Son! Angels sang in the distance, "Glory to God in the highest and on earth peace, good will to all."

Sometime later, wise men came with their gifts of gold, frankincense and myrrh. *(With regret)* But soon, our celebration ended. Herod became furious when he learned of the Christ child's birth. We had to escape for our lives into Egypt and remain there until Herod's death.

(Pensively) On returning to Nazareth, a note of sadness settled upon my soul, as the words of Isaiah kept echoing in my mind. "He was wounded for our transgression. He was bruised for our iniquity. The chastisement of our peace was upon him and by his stripes we are healed."

I kept wondering what lay ahead for the Christ child. Whatever it was, God was doing a marvelous thing for his people. Although it would be filled with pain for God's dear Son, it would bring peace to receptive hearts. *(Spends a few moments in thoughtful silence.)*

(Pointedly to audience) May I leave you with two thoughts? One is that I am grateful to God for allowing me to be the guardian of his Son. Although I was much in the background, he gave me a part in salvation's drama. No matter how small your godly efforts may seem, God can make them a mighty ministry.

A second thought is that God has done all of this for you. Just as I am in the picture of your Nativity scene, you are in it too, because God so loved you *(He begins his exit)* that he gave his only begotten Son . . .

David

DAVID, THE SHEPHERD KING
I Samuel 16:10-13; Psalm 23

Often described as "a man after God's own heart," David indeed pursued the heart of his Lord throughout an adventure-filled life. Gratefully, he shared his joys and triumphs with God, who was their giver. Humbly, he begged forgiveness from God, who authored his pardon. Eagerly, he sought the will of God, who guided his steps through a military career to the kingship of Israel. While David was never one to be devastated by failures or immobilized by mistakes, he apparently spent much time in his advancing years remembering earlier days. Psalm 23 makes an excellent point of reference as we listen to the Shepherd King reminisce.

Props: None needed

Delivery time: 20-26 minutes

(DAVID enters reciting the 23rd Psalm.) **"The Lord is my Shepherd, I shall not want. He maketh me to lie down in green pastures, he leadeth me beside the still waters; he restoreth my soul. He leadeth me in the paths of righteousness for his name's sake. Yea, though I walk through the valley of the shadow of death, I will fear no evil. Thy rod and thy staff, they comfort me. Thou preparest a table before me in the presence of mine enemies. Thou anointest my head with oil; my cup runneth over. Surely, goodness and mercy shall follow me all the days of my life, and I shall dwell in the house of the Lord forever."**

(Short pause; addresses audience.) **Perhaps you think that as a young man I composed this poem while I sat among my father's sheep. But no, it was in my later years when I grew to see how God had been more than adequate in all the trying circumstances of my life. He had designed all my recoveries. He was the author of all my blessings.**

There was no doubting the fact that he was the Shepherd of my life. As an older man, I was able to understand this truth from the perspective of all my years. God's hand had been upon me all the way. The excitement of that fact brought comfort to my declining days. It inspired every creative faculty of my being as I wrote this hymn of personal praise and worship. My poem, which you call the 23rd Psalm, caused me to remember all the episodes of my life in which God was the moving force.

(Pauses to collect thoughts; speaks enthusiastically.) I never will forget the day Samuel visited our home. I was but a lad with the fascinating chore of keeping the sheep. I enjoyed my contribution to the family farm. In fact, I was rather good at it. I understood sheep, and they understood me.

You know, sheep are a lot like people. They worry and fret. They frolic and play. They balk and rebel. What a challenge! Everybody ought to be a shepherd at least once in life.

It was a resting period when my father's servant came requesting that I return home for an audience with Samuel.

(Fondly) He was a grand old man. The spirit of God was upon him mightily. I felt as though I was talking to God, himself. At the time, I didn't grasp all that Samuel was saying. He talked about the sins of King Saul and how God was not going to let him rule much longer. He told me that one day I would replace him.

Although I respected Samuel, I certainly did not conceive of myself as being the king of Israel. To be honest with you, at that stage in my life, I was much more interested in being a shepherd than in being a king.

(With a sense of wonder) Although I did not fully comprehend the meaning of those moments, I was never

the same again. It was like conversion! When Samuel laid his hands on me and anointed me with oil, something like the power of God poured into every part of my being. From that day forth, I was a different man. The Lord had anointed my head with oil, and my cup was running over!

(Excitedly) The next few years of my life were filled with drama, danger and difficulty. Although I had received the anointing of God, there was no indication that life was going to be easy. As I look back upon it, the greatest tests of my life followed the call of God. Isn't it strange how God calls and then proceeds to push our faith and stamina to the breaking point?

(Recalls with sadness.) It was a sad and gloomy day when I took supplies to my soldier brothers in the valley of Elah. Not only were the Philistines a formidable foe, but they had a giant named Goliath. He proposed that someone from Israel face him in a one-on-one conflict. The winner would determine the outcome of the battle between the two nations.

Now, no one from Israel was a match for his herculean strength. There was a dilemma. What could Israel do?

(With growing excitement) When I heard about it, I had this strange urge to accept the giant's challenge. After all, I had encountered bears and lions in my role as a shepherd. Perhaps I could do as well with this overgrown Philistine! Everyone, especially my brothers, discouraged my ridiculous offer to fight Goliath. In fact, even I didn't cherish the idea of facing that oversized human being!

(With confidence and pride) However, the spirit of God was urging me to accept the assignment. Yea, though I walked through that valley of the shadow of possible death, I did not fear because God was with me. I claimed victory that day over Goliath and the Philistines in the name of the Lord God of Israel!

(Seriously again) **Goliath was but a symbol of the giants I faced in those years of my early manhood.**

King Saul, who had elevated me to a place of prominence in his court, turned against me. On one occasion, he actually tried to kill me! Had it not been for Jonathan later, I would not have escaped Saul's evil conspiracy to have me killed. Because of Saul's sinister plans, I was compelled to live for years as an outlaw in his eyes. Every day I feared for my life as I was pursued like a common criminal by his men.

(Wearily) **Those were hectic days when often I could have killed King Saul myself. As it was, I narrowly escaped his own sword.**

However, some positive things did come from those turbulent days. I was able to organize an effective fighting force of several hundred men. I became close friends of my people in the southern part of Israel. I grew through every obstacle to see that God was preparing me to be the king of Israel. In every danger I faced, it seemed as though the Lord prepared a table before me in the presence of my enemies.

Although I had suffered much at the hand of Saul, it was not a happy day when I learned of his death. Even in his madness, Saul was still the anointed of God. I respected his divinely appointed office, and I loved his family.

The Lord led me to Hebron, where I was anointed king over the house of Judah. Over seven years I ruled in Judah until Ishbosheth, the son of Saul, was slain. Then I was asked to be king over all of Israel.

(Proudly, but not boastfully) **The Lord was with me, and I established the holy city of Jerusalem as the capital. My armies defeated our enemies and stretched our boundaries in all directions. From all over the world we brought precious materials to build the palaces of**

Jerusalem. The Lord God Jehovah had made us the strongest nation on earth! Our power and wealth were unlimited!

(With longing) I wanted desperately to build God's temple, but my hands were stained with blood because I was a warrior king. Nonetheless, goodness and mercy were following me.

(With regret) My success and prosperity had a damaging effect upon my ego. As a proud king, I felt I could do as I pleased and get what I wanted. In lust one day I coveted another man's wife and proceeded in a murderous plan to get what I wanted. *(Mocking himself)* After all, I was the king! Who could deny my request? But I soon learned life was not designed that way, even for kings.

(Shame makes speaking difficult.) It was a painful day when Nathan came to me with his parable of accusation. Not only was it embarrassing to learn my sin was known, it was difficult to confront the many awkward implications of my misbehavior. It especially hurt to realize I had grieved the heart of God.

The words of Nathan, "Thou are the man," cut a clear, clean path to the core of my being. With remorse in my heart, I admitted my error to Nathan.

In my secret place of prayer, I cried unto the Lord: *(Falls to knees and prays fervently.)* "Have mercy on me, O God, according to thy loving kindness. According to thy great compassion, blot out my transgressions. Wash me thoroughly from my iniquity and cleanse me from my sin. For I know my transgressions, and my sin is ever before me. Against thee and thee only have I sinned and done this evil in thy sight. Purge me with hyssop and I shall be clean. Wash me and I shall be whiter than snow.

(Tearfully; with deep emotion) "Make me to hear joy and gladness. Let the bones which thou hast broken rejoice.

Hide thy face from my sins and blot out all my iniquities. Create in me a clean heart, O God, and renew a right spirit within me. Do not cast me away from thy presence. And do not take thy Holy Spirit from me. Restore to me the joy of thy salvation and sustain me with a willing spirit."

(Regains composure; rises slowly; speaks with wonder and gratitude.) You know, the Lord forgave my sin! He removed the burden of my guilt, and I praise him! I praise him! There is a balm in Gilead, a healing fountain." How blessed is he whose transgression is forgiven, whose sin is covered! How blessed is the person to whom the Lord does not charge iniquity and in whose spirit there is no deceit!"

Surley, surely he restored my soul and led me in the paths of righteousness for his name's sake.

(With deepening sadness) While my sins were forgiven, the strains of my transgressions marred the tapestry of my life for years to come. I loved my family dearly, but they did not love one another. Perhaps they followed me to the far country of sin, and when I returned, they remained in the land of disobedience.

In it all, I learned the painful lesson that, although God beautifully forgives sin, even he does not rub out the consequences of iniquity. What pain it brought to my heart to have my own daughter raped by my own son, then to have that son murdered by his brother!

What grief it produced in my declining years to see my beloved country torn by civil war led by my own son, Absalom! I thought my heart would break in two when they told me of Absalom's death.

(With much anguish) Oh, Absalom, my son, my son, Absalom, that I had died instead of you! Oh, Absalom, if only I had set a better example! If only I had nurtured you in your youth! If only I had won your love as a young man! Oh, Absalom, Absalom, my dear, dear son!

How could I stand to see my sons and others compete for my throne? *(Regaining composure)* **With Nathan, my trusted friend and spiritual advisor, we selected and anointed Solomon to be my successor so there could be peace in our land again.**

(Sadly) **Many times during those turbulent days I wanted to escape. I longed for the wings of a dove so I might fly away and be at rest. Deep down, however, I knew life was not made for flight but for facing each challenge with courage and composure.**

After all, the Lord was my Shepherd. He was making me to lie down in green pastures and leading me beside still waters. *(Joyfully)* **Hallelujah, what a Shepherd! I commend him to you today.**

(Moves closer to audience; speaks solemnly.) **Looking down the corridors of time, I see my Shepherd again, the Messiah of God, Jesus Christ, God's only Son. By word and deed, he revealed he was the good Shepherd who laid down his life for his sheep.**

Today, he is the door to that eternal sheep fold. He wants to let you in. Will you seek him? Will you commit yourself to this Shepherd, this Christ of God? Will you come to him? If you will come today, you can say with me, the Lord is my Shepherd, I shall not want. *(He exits, again reciting the 23rd Psalm.)*

Elijah

ELIJAH
I Kings 18:17-39

Elijah is another great man of God who wonderfully exhibits human traits. While he was a prophet with a keen ear for the voice of the Lord, he was also a man who repeatedly battled fear. He boldly proclaimed bad news to a pagan king, then fled for his life into the wilderness for divine protection. He longed to stay in the comfort and security of his brookside retreat when God sent him back to work in the world. Even the mighty miracles he called forth from Jehovah could not keep him from running away from a vengeful queen. Still, Elijah conquered his fears and allowed God to use him as he had used no other prophet.

Props: None needed (ELIJAH's costume needs an easily removable "mantle," or cape-like garment.)

Delivery time: 20-25 minutes

(ELIJAH enters; focuses his attention Stage Left or Right and speaks authoritatively, as if someone else is there.) **Listen to my words, O King Ahab! As the Lord, the God of Israel lives, before whom I stand, there shall be no rain nor dew these years, except by my word.**

King Ahab, why have you become enamored with this strange god? Why have you allowed Jezebel to lead the people away from the God of Israel to worship Baal? The Lord our God is the one who controls the seasons, the planting and the harvest. He is the Lord God of the weather, and to prove it, he is going to withhold the rain to show you his sovereign power.

(Turns to audience.) **I know you are wondering who I am to be talking** *(Gestures in direction of earlier focus)* **to the king like this! Well, I am Elijah, the Tishbite from Gilead. The Lord called me to be his prophet, his spokesman, at a crucial time in the history of Israel. Therefore, let me share with you some of the fascinating details of my life.**

Of course, the king was upset by my words, and I had to leave immediately. He disliked my reminder of the Lord God of Israel more than he believed my prediction. He must have laughed for days at the ridiculous words of this strange prophet. Yet, as the rainless weeks turned into months, he became furious and began to search diligently for me.

God, however, had prepared a place for me beside the brook, Kerith. *(Contently)* Here I was fed by the ravens and drank from the brook. I had it made! I enjoyed sitting by the stream, bathing in its bright beauty and refreshing flow. The land was drying up, but I had my brook, my sparkling, cooling brook.

(Incredulously) But then one day, it dried up. Can you imagine God drying up my brook? What would I do? Had God brought me here to die?

No. God had something more for me to do than piously enjoy his provisions, while the people around perished from the drought. The brook was only a temporary blessing to encourage my faith and strengthen my body for future responsibilities. It was not to be a style of life.

(Pointedly to audience) We all have brooks which dry up. How long has it been since some disappointment, some heartache or some loss has left you wondering about God's care? I know how you feel. I greatly grieved over my brook and felt God had forsaken me. However, in the midst of my turmoil, I heard the call to go to Zarephath. Then I understood the gospel of the dry brook. Why, I would have stayed there forever! God had to force me out. I could not have heard his call amid the comfort and security of my brook.

(Gently) Neither can you. Perhaps God is drying up your brook to lead you to some Zarephath. Your anguish and pain may be the conditions under which God can call

you and use you in a more effective way. Listen, if your brook has never dried up, sooner or later it will. Be prepared to hear the voice of God, or you will never find your way to Zarephath.

At Zarephath, I found a hungry widow who was willing to share her last bit of meal and oil with me. In fact, when I first saw her, she was preparing to serve this only remaining food before she and her son died of starvation. Having shared with me, I told her that the Lord God of Israel would not let her run out of meal and oil until he would send rain upon the earth. For many days, we all ate from her supply, and it was not depleted.

In case you do not recall, Zarephath was a Phoenician city. *(With excitement)* Here, I was able to take the word of the Lord God of Israel to the country of Jezebel, to the very heart of Baalism itself. My big opportunity came when the widow's son died. She blamed his death on my presence. However, I prayed to God, and the Lord restored his life. Afterward, she gave my God the credit for his resurrected life. Now she knew the words of my mouth were true. Jehovah had won a victory in the land of Baal. I learned that if God could use me in Zarephath, he could use me anywhere.

So it is with you. You may think there are places too difficult for God to use you to witness. Not so! There is no situation so sinful God cannot redeem it. There is no circumstance so painful God cannot heal it. There are no people so indifferent that God cannot arouse in them an interest. Listen. If God has called you to your own Zarephath, be aware that his miracles are about to begin.

(Pauses to collect thoughts.) One of the major events of my life began as God sent me to Ahab with word that he would send rain on the earth once again. Ahab was still searching for me. He had inquired everywhere about me. I learned there was a price on my head. I had no way of

knowing how Ahab would react when he saw me. After all, he was the king. I met Obadiah on my way, and he was fearful for his life. Because of the king's fury, he was afraid to tell him I was even in the area.

(With much animation) The land was parched and dry, and when I met King Ahab, he was hot and angry. "Is that you, you troublemaker of Israel?" he said to me.

"Troublemaker?" I said. "You are the troublemaker! You are the one who has forsaken the commandments of God and caused the people to follow Baal. Now God has withheld the rain to teach you, O King, that he is the Lord of Israel!"

I told the king if he wanted me to prove the Lord Jehovah was the true God, we would have a contest on Mt. Carmel. He agreed to gather the four hundred fifty prophets of Baal and the four hundred prophets of Asherah with all the people on the mountain. When everyone was assembled, I demanded, "How long will you falter between two opinions? If the Lord Jehovah is God, then follow him, but if Baal, then follow him." *(Very quietly)* There was silence. No one said a word.

Next, I made a proposal. "Let us take two bulls. You prophets of Baal, prepare your bull on your altar for sacrifice, and I'll prepare mine on my altar for sacrifice. We will put no fire to it, but will call on our separate gods for fire. The god who answers, let him be our god!"

They agreed and began to call on Baal. All morning long they called to Baal, but there was no answer. *(Sarcastically)* I asked them to cry louder. Perhaps their god was on a journey or perhaps asleep. The prophets of Baal became frantic. They cried loudly, they danced, they cut themselves with swords until blood gushed out!

(With distaste) It was pitiful to see people get so worked up over a false god. But there was no voice. No one answered. Nothing happened. It is awful for people to

commit themselves to a god that cannot save. It is horrible to wake up one day to find that time and energy has been spent on gods we have created rather than on the God who created us. Is there a lesson here for all of us?

After the prophets of Baal had spent themselves, I prepared the altar of the Lord God of Israel. *(With growing anticipation)* I placed the sacrifice upon it and requested that twelve jars of water be poured all over the altar. Then I prayed to the Lord God of Abraham, Isaac and Israel. I said, "Let these people this day know that you alone are God and that I am your prophet and these are your words!"

(With wonder and excitement) Then the great miracle happened! The fire of the Lord fell from heaven and consumed the sacrifice, the wood, the stone altar and even the water! There was nothing left but the fact that God was in that place.

When the people saw this, they fell on their faces and cried, "The Lord, he is God! The Lord, he is God!"

This was another exciting episode in my life! Now, the people believed that Jehovah was the Lord of Israel! He is the Lord God of the rain, the weather and the crops!

(Triumphantly) When the prophets of Baal realized what had happened, they tried to escape. But the people seized them and executed them for causing the name of God to be desecrated in Israel.

After this, I told Ahab to eat and drink because rain was coming. I prayed to God on Mt. Carmel. Six times I sent my servant to observe the weather conditions, and he saw nothing. On the seventh time, he saw a small cloud. I then told Ahab to get his chariot and go down off the mountain, because the rain was near. He left, and in a little while there were dark clouds, thunder, lightning, wind and then rain! A great rain!

(Joyfully) I felt wonderful! Now I knew God had won

the victory, and I would be established as his prophet! I even envisioned Jezebel giving me a place of recognition in her court. *(With amazement)* How wrong I was! She was furious and . . . and even threatened my life! She decreed to have me killed by the next day.

(Fearfully) I was afraid. Oh, I was afraid! I fled immediately with my servant. We hardly stopped until we came to Beersheba. I left my servant there and traveled into the wilderness alone for another day. I collapsed under a juniper tree saying, *(Despondently)* "Lord, I am weary! I can't fight any longer. I thought we had the victory, but apparently we did not. It is enough, O Lord. Take away my life! Just . . . let me die."

I must have fallen asleep, because I was awakened by an angel. He fed me and strengthened me for my journey to Mt. Horeb. As you know, Mt. Horeb is sometimes called Sinai where Moses received the Law of God.

At Horeb, the word of the Lord came to me telling me to go forth and stand on the mountain, and the Lord would pass by. *(Loudly; with excitement and gestures)* When I did, there was a mighty wind that broke the rocks and shook the mountain, but the Lord was not in the wind. After the wind, there was a mighty earthquake, but the Lord was not in it either. Then there was a blazing fire, but the Lord was not in the fire. *(Quietly)* Finally, there was a still, small voice, and when I heard it, I wrapped my face in my mantle and stood near the entrance of my cave. The voice said, "What are you doing here, Elijah?"

(Defensively) I answered, "I am here because I have been very zealous for you, the Lord God of Israel! Because Israel has forsaken your covenant, torn down the altar and slain the prophets. I, only I am left. They seek my life to take it away."

The Lord said to me, "Go! Go back, Elijah! I have more

for you to do. First, go to the wilderness of Damascus. From there, you shall anoint Hazael to be king of Syria, Jehu to be king of Israel. Anoint Elisha, son of Shaphat, to be a prophet in your place. Listen, Elijah, there are seven thousand in Israel who have not bowed their knees to Baal. I am not through with Baalism! I am not through with Ahab and wicked Jezebel."

(Emphatically) And he was not! For years, violence prevailed in Israel until Ahab, Jezebel and all the followers of Baal met with tragedy and death.

It was my happy privilege to find Elisha, who was plowing twelve yoke of oxen. *(With admiration)* I called him to follow me, and so great was his willingness and commitment that he killed the oxen, boiled their flesh and fed it to the people. He made a complete break with farming to become a prophet. He wanted nothing to distract him from being God's spokesman. What an example of absolute dedication!

Elisha needed this kind of rugged faith for the ministry God called him to perform. Every generation needs this kind of commitment. *(Firmly)* What is there in your life which needs to be forsaken so you can be all God is calling you to be? Learn from Elisha what it means to put God first in your life.

Elisha was a good man and a faithful companion to me. *(With a growing sense of wonder)* One day, I had a strange feeling that something wonderful was going to happen. I felt as though God had finished his work through me. Elisha must have felt the same way because he followed me wherever I went. Finally, I stopped and asked Elisha what I could do for him. He said, "Give me a double portion of your spirit."

I told him, "If you are with me when I depart this earth, it will be a sign that you shall have your desire."

We walked on beyond Jordan, suddenly there was

a fiery chariot and horses before me! *(Excitedly)* **Then a power like a whirlwind took me** *(Begins removing mantle)* **up from the earth into the presence of God! My mantle fell,** *(Lets mantle slip to floor)* **and as I looked back, Elisha was picking it up.**

(Pauses; shakes head, as if to clear mind.) **I cannot tell you any more because your minds would not be able to grasp the glory of God and the wonderful things he has in store for his faithful servants.**

I can tell you, however, about the greatest thing that ever happened to me. You call the place the Mount of Transfiguration. Jesus took Peter, James and John up on a high mountain. There, God allowed Moses and me to visit his Son. We came to offer encouragement as he faced his cross. We came representing the law and the prophets, which for years had looked to him for fulfillment. *(With awe)* **It was a glorious thing for me to behold the Lamb of God who takes away the sins of the world! The most important thing about this event was not our presence, but the voice of God who said, "This is my beloved Son, in whom I am well pleased. Hear ye him! Hear ye him!"**

(Moves closer to audience.) **Today, you have been listening to me relate the details of my life. It is well that you know me and how God used me, yet it is more important that you know this Jesus, who is Christ. Hear ye him! Hear him who said, "Come unto me all ye that labor and are heavy laden." Hear him who said, "Behold, I stand at the door and knock. If any man hear my voice and open the door, I will come in to him and will sup with him and he with me." Hear him who said, "If any man would come after me, let him deny himself, take up his cross and follow me."**

(Gently, reverently) **Yes, it is good to listen to Elijah. But it is much better to listen to the Christ and his offer of salvation, which is possible for all who will believe on his name.** *(He exits.)*

John

JOHN, THE BELOVED DISCIPLE
I John 1:1-10

John's gospel reveals a particular attentiveness to Jesus and an eagerness to understand the man and his mission. It is significant that he was called "beloved," but we must be careful not to interpret that as meaning "favorite." Perhaps John's deep, sincere curiosity about Jesus' purpose and personality inspired what John felt to be a little more emotional intimacy with him than the others. In any event, John was the portrait painter of our Lord, and this monolog was written to communicate the "I am" declarations as told by one who heard them firsthand.

Props: None needed
Delivery time: 20-23 minutes

(JOHN could be speaking from Off-Stage. If On-Stage, his attitude is one of musing, a soliloquy not directed to the audience.) **"In the beginning was the Word, and the Word was with God, and the Word was God. The same was in the beginning with God.**

"All things were made by him, and without him was not anything made that was made. In him was life, and the life was the light of men. And the light shineth in the darkness, and the darkness comprehended it not.

"And the Word became flesh and dwelt among us, and we beheld his glory, the glory of the only begotten of the Father, full of grace and truth."

(There is a short silence. JOHN comes On-Stage or turns toward the audience and speaks tenderly.) **It's a long way from the boats of Capernaum to the heights of Mount Transfiguration. It's a long way from the smelly nets of Galilee to the miraculous ministry of the Galilean.**

It's a long way from the quiet, peaceful stillness of fishing waters to the rambling, ranting rage of Golgotha's hill. It's a long way from the comforts of a respected

family setting to the prison of Patmos Isle. It's a long way from being the son of Zebedee to being the beloved disciple.

(Still gently, with a hint of wonder) **But now you may ask, "What made the distance and what made the difference?"**

I will tell you. The difference and the distance was Jesus. Only Jesus could have changed my life in the ways it was changed. Only the Word made flesh could have brought about such a dramatic turn of events. Only the Christ of God could have made such a difference in my thinking, my actions, and my whole lifestyle.

(More forcefully) **Although the difference Jesus brought to me was profound and spiritually profitable, it was not a life of ease to which I had been called. There were times of sadness as well as joy, moments of fear as well as faith, events of failure as well as success, reactions of hate as well as love.**

It was a long way from where I was to where he wanted me to be. For you see, I was a turbulent, ambitious and intolerant young man, who often needed the reproof of my Lord. Yet, in his love he allowed me to abide. Because of his love, I was able to grow, and on the strength of his love, I learned to love him and to love the brethren.

Yes, I am the beloved disciple, not because of my great capacity to love but because of his willingness to share his love through me.

(Waves away the feeling of reverie and speaks enthusiastically.) **Enough! Enough about me! Let me tell you about the one who made such a difference in me. Let me tell you about this only begotten of the Father, full of grace and truth. Let me tell you about this Lamb of God who takes away the sin of the world.**

He is the one who called Nicodemus from the drudgery of tradition and invited him to share a new birth. He is the one who sat with a Samaritan woman of ill repute on the rim of Jacob's well. He allowed her to drink the water of acceptance and love until she became enthralled by his Messianic possibilities.

He is the one who cleansed the temple, healed by the pool of Bethesda, gave sight to a man born blind, walked on the water and gave people a lesson every time he talked. *(Imploringly)* Surely, he is worthy of your attention today!

(Sadly) One of the things that grieved my Lord the most was that people did not understand who he was and what he had come to do. On several occasions, Jesus gave us profound insights into his divine character and purpose. *(Brightening)* Usually during these moments of self-revelation, he would summarize his intended truth and begin with the words, "I am."

When Jesus began a statement with "I am," I listened with keen anticipation because I knew he was going to share a tender truth about himself. I pondered these "I am" sayings and included them in my gospel. In many ways, they formed the basis of my understanding of who he was and what he came to do. Perhaps they can be equally significant to you.

It was a beautiful day near Galilee when thousands of people congregated on the hillside to hear Jesus teach and watch him do miracles of healing. But words and miracles, fascinating though they be, do not fill empty stomachs. The people became hungry and needed to eat.

Therefore, Jesus performed his most impressive miracle of the day. *(Excitedly, with amazement)* He took five barley loaves and two small fish and fed the entire multitude! It was a fantastic gesture which excited the people. Not only could this man heal them, he could feed them! He had the power to give them whatever they needed. They wanted him for their king. You should have seen their enthusiasm!

(More calmly) **Now, Jesus knew they misunderstood. He tried to explain that he had not come to feed hungry bodies but to feed starving souls. In his attempt to address their deeper hunger, he came forth with the words, "I am the bread of life. He that cometh to me shall not hunger."**

Something deeper than physical hunger had captured his attention. He was soul food sent from heaven to fill the emptiness and to heal the heartsickness of all whose sins jeopardized their happiness. Oh, yes, Jesus is the bread of life. He was for me, and he can be for you.

(Pause for remembering) **I remember the last Feast of the Tabernacles which Jesus attended. I especially remember the night of the Illumination of the Temple. The great candelabra was lit and sent its shining rays all over the city. It was to be a time of celebration and praise,** *(Sadly)* **but there was little for us Jews to celebrate. Our country had been bludgeoned into submission by a despot.**

There was a darkness in our land even the great candelabra could not illumine. Oh, how fitting it was for Jesus to emerge and say, *(Quoted with confidence)* **"I am the light of the world; he who follows me shall not walk in darkness but shall have the light of life."**

Jesus brought a sense of illumination and revelation about ourselves and about God that we had never known before. He was the light shining the love of God upon our souls.

(With slight impatience) **My fellow countrymen became angry with Jesus because he claimed such intimate fellowship with the heavenly Father. They could not understand how any earthly person could be greater than their father, Abraham. It was inconceivable to them that Abraham was in any way related to this Jesus of Nazareth. Yet, in the midst of their confusion and rejection of his**

godliness, Jesus proposed that "before Abraham was, I am."

By this time, I was fearful because they picked up stones to throw at him. I could not understand their blindness! *(Defensively)* All he was saying was what I said earlier: "In the beginning was the Word." Whatever he was like was the way God had always been. His plan of saving a lost world was God's plan from the beginning. He was the timeless Christ who came to change our few years of time into eternity.

(Pause) It was a day for parables, and I listened intently as Jesus talked about sheep and shepherds. Although I had never been involved in the shepherding business, I had always admired these men of the field. They seemed to demonstrate such patience, such leadership, such devotion and such courage, even to the point of risking everything for the sake of the sheep.

It seemed appropriate that he should say, "I am the good shepherd who lays down his life for the sheep. I am the good shepherd and know my own, and my own know me."

(Slightly humorously) In many ways, our disciple band was a tender flock, but oh, what a motley crew we were for his shepherding skills! Like sheep of the field, we would have gone our own way had it not been for this shepherd of God. *(Pensively)* As I pondered his shepherdship, I wondered, could ever there be a sheep so lost that a saving shepherd like him could not find it?

(Pauses to recall another incident; portrays confusion.) Lazarus was sick and apparently sick unto death. Because they were such good friends, I could not understand why Jesus did not hasten to be with him. At first, I thought he lingered because of the Jews who threatened to stone him. But later he said, "Let's go. Our friend Lazarus is dead." And we followed, even though the risk was great.

Martha was so upset when we arrived. "Lord, why have you lingered?" she cried to him. "If only you had been here, my dear brother would not have died! Why? Why?"

Jesus calmly assured her Lazarus would rise again. Of course, Martha believed that would be so on the last day, but it did not relieve her need for her brother then.

At this point of frustration and hurt, Jesus gave us another profound insight into his being. "I am the resurrection and the life; he who believes in me, though he die, yet shall he live. And whosoever lives and believes in me shall never die."

Of course, we did not understand all he was saying at the time. Later, we gradually grew to understand that where Jesus is there is resurrection and there is life. Such things as the raising of Lazarus and his own glorious resurrection gave us reasons to defy the death-threatening opposition we faced as we sought to build his church.

(Pause for more recollection) Those were precious moments in the upper room with Jesus. The last supper lingered lovingly in our minds as we pondered the great truths he gave us. In an effort to prepare us for his departure, he assured us that his going was in our best interest. He assumed we knew where he was going and the way he was going.

But Thomas did not know. He was much too honest and sincere to remain silent about his ignorance. "Lord, we do not know where, and we do not know the way. Tell us more!" he pleaded.

Gently, Jesus responded to him, "Thomas, I am the way, the truth and the life; no one comes to the Father but by me. All you really need to know is me, Thomas. Knowing me you know the way to God, the truth of God, and life everlasting."

(With relief) What comfort it brought to his doubtful mind, when Thomas was able to see that Jesus was the answer to his kind of questions!

And so it was for all of us. Jesus knew that not only Thomas but all of us were uneasy about the future. He knew we all needed something to which we could cling for stability and strength.

We know too much and our assignments were far too demanding to think we could do it on our own. Imagine what music it was to our intimidated talents to hear him say, "I am the vine; you are the branches. He that abideth in me and I in him, the same bringeth forth much fruit. For without me, you can do nothing."

In other words, we were his, and he was ours, and there was nothing outside the realm of possibility, nothing outside the scope of God's redeemability.

(With growing animation) Now, do you see why I get so excited when I talk about him? He is the Word made flesh, the Lily of the Valley, the bright and morning star, the great "I am."

(With increasing sadness) Joyous though we were with our Lord, the moments of arrest, trial, and crucifixion were terrifying indeed.

(With great distaste at morbid memories) Crucifixion. Oh, it was an ugly scene! Too cruel for loving hearts. His mother and I were there simply to give him friendly faces in the anguish of death. Looking down with blood-spattered eyes and speaking through fevered lips, he said, "Woman, behold your son. Son, behold your mother."

What confidence and love he expressed in assigning me the care of the one who gave birth and nurture to the Son of God!

(Pauses; shakes head in wonder, then brightens with a new idea.) But you know something? He has a similar assignment for you! Listen to him as he says, "Behold one another. You are church, you are fellowship. You belong to one another because you belong to me. Care one for another."

(Emphatically, excitedly) **Listen to him as he says, "Behold my world. Go! Go! Go, and share my love, and lo, I will be with you."**

Listen to him as he says, "Behold, I stand at the door and knock. If anyone opens, I will come in and dine with him."

(Pauses; moves closer to the audience; speaks imploringly.) **Do you have that kind of fellowship? If not, do you want it? Then come to Jesus. It's imperative that you do! I was given a vision of the great judgment of God, and those whose names were not in the Book of Life were cast into a lake of fire.**

(JOHN begins his exit, then turns back to audience.) **Behold! He says, "Come!"**

Jonah

JONAH, THE RELUCTANT MISSIONARY
Jonah 1:1-3; 3:10; 4:11

While Jonah earned his fame as a reluctant missionary, his story also contains lessons on selfishness, pride, disobedience, love and God's dependence upon imperfect human beings. He is hardheaded and knows it, contrite and admits it, narrow-minded and prays about it. For a prophet, he seems somewhat ignorant of God's capacities, or else his distaste for his assignment obliterated what wisdom he possessed. Perhaps it was a sense of humor which helped him emerge from his terrifying boat ride and unique confinement with more than an "okay, okay, I'll go," response. Grateful as we all are for a second chance, Jonah made a success of his revival in Nineveh. But again, his preoccupation with self kept him from participating fully in his role as a channel of God's grace.

Props: None needed
Delivery time: 18-20 minutes

(He enters at rear of assembly, preaching loudly and forcefully as he comes forward.) **Forty days, Nineveh! Yes, forty days and Nineveh shall be destroyed!** *(Faces left or right, but not the audience.)* **Oh, you people of Nineveh, do you now know that the Lord, Jehovah, is God? He is the judge of all the earth and your wickedness is known to him! He is a righteous God and he will not tolerate your evil ways.** *(Emphatic, pleading)* **He requires you to repent and turn from your sin. If not, a great nation from the east will overrun your cities and devour your land.** *(Still not facing audience)* **Listen, forty days! Oh, Nineveh, just forty days!** *(Loud again)* **God is giving you forty days, and if you do not humble yourselves and seek him, his wrath will fall upon you! Remember, Nineveh,** *(Voice fades)* **forty days . . . forty days . . .**

(Prayerful pause; turns toward and "discovers" audience; speaks conversationally.) **Oh, hello there. I'm Jonah, the son**

of Amittai from Gath Hepher. I have been on a preaching mission to Nineveh, of all places. I have a most unusual story to tell you that you may find difficult to believe. First of all, I want to tell you that my story is not about me. It's not necessarily a story about a fish. It's not even a story about Nineveh. The truth is, mine is a story about God. Keep in mind that the God who sent me to Nineveh is a God of miracles.

(With pride) I was a prophet in Israel during the reign of Jeroboam, II. I was a popular preacher. I predicted good things for Israel. You can read about me in II Kings 14:25. God helped to restore the borders of Israel, and he used me to make the proclamation.

(Satisfied, almost cocky) I had it made. I was comfortable. God blessed my message. I had quite a reputation as a prophet. I was well liked. Then one day God asked me to go to Nineveh. Can you imagine that? *(With disbelief)* I was just beginning to enjoy the popularity and prestige of being Israel's leading prophet when God called me — *me* — to go to Nineveh!

(With exaggerated patience) Now, perhaps you do not know what it meant to go to Nineveh in those days. You see, Nineveh was the capital of Assyria. Assyria was our big, big enemy. It was like asking *(Supply name familiar to audience)* to go to Moscow or *(Another familiar name)* to Peking and tell them of their wickedness!

(Shakes head; makes gesture of refusal.) Nineveh was not for me. I wanted no part of that assignment. So, I thought I would just ignore the call, but I couldn't. Every time the wind blew, it whispered my call. *(Softly, almost singing)* "Jonah, go to Nineveh!"

Every time the thunder crashed, it punctuated the sovereignty of God who had given me this task. The birds sang about it. *(Gestures widely.)* Everywhere I turned, the still, small voice of God pursued me.

Finally, I had all I could take. I had to get out of Israel. I assumed that if I could only get out of Israel, I could get away from the presence of the Lord. If I could go to another land, I felt I could avoid everything that reminded me of his call. I offered my resignation as a prophet and decided to get as far away from Israel and Nineveh as I could.

In my plan to get away from God, I bought a ticket on a ship sailing for Tarshish. This was on the other end of the Great Sea. As I boarded the ship, it felt good to be getting out of the country. I went straight to my bunk and went to sleep. After all, I had not slept in days. I could sleep now that I was out of the land of Jehovah. *(With contempt)* God would have to call someone else to go to Nineveh or else give up on his strange notion of saving those heathen infidels!

It seemed I had been asleep only for a little while when someone was shaking me. "Wake up," they said. "Wake up and pray to your God! We are in a terrible storm!"

Sleepily, I found my way to the place where the crew and passengers had gathered in great fear. Someone shouted, *(Fearfully)* "Who has done evil toward their god, causing him to send this storm upon us?"

Another said, "Let's cast lots, so we may know who is guilty."

Of course, the lot fell on me. It was at this moment I began to realize I could not run away from God.

The men asked me a lot of questions. *(With resignation)* For me, it was confession time. I told them I was a Hebrew, and I served the Lord, Jehovah, who had made heaven, earth and sea. I explained that I was fleeing from his presence, because he had called me to go to Nineveh. "I am the cause of the storm," I told them. "It is my sin which has angered God."

As the storm worsened, the men became frantic. "What shall we do with you?" they asked.

As I looked at these sailors, I realized they did not deserve to share my judgment. They had not participated in my disobedience. "Throw me overboard," I suggested. "Then the sea will be calm. The wrath of God will be appeased, and you can continue your journey in peace."

(With amazement) I could not believe the compassion of these men. Could Gentiles really care for me, a Hebrew? They would not throw me over. They rowed harder and harder, trying to reach land before they disposed of me.

But it was no use. The Lord God of Israel, the God of the sea, had other plans for me. The men had no alternative but to cast me into the water. They did not want to do it, but I insisted. What was happening to me? Even though those sailors were not of my race, I had concern for them. I did not want to see them perish. Isn't it ironic that while I had been unwilling to go to the thousands at Nineveh, I was now willing to be sacrificed to the sea for a handful of pagans? *(With disbelief)* I was actually willing to die that others might live.

While praying to my God, those sympathetic seamen tossed me overboard, asking for divine favor and forgiveness of their inhuman deed. God was with them, and God was with me. As I hit the sea, I could feel calm come upon the waters. The storm was over. A proud and disobedient preacher had reversed his flight from God. I went down . . . down . . . down . . . expecting life to leave me at any moment. But it didn't. *(With amazement)* Suddenly, I found myself in a dark, slick, slimy cavity. Nothing but blackness! Oh, so dark. I finally realized I was in the stomach of a great fish!

(Emphatically) I'll tell you, I really began to pray! The slimy darkness was not a fit place to think, much less pray.

The thunderous pounding of the fish's heart and its constant motion punished me unbearably. *(In desperation)* Darkness, darkness! Nothing but indescribable blackness! Never had I felt so alone! "Out!" I cried to God. "Let me out of this belly . . . this . . . this hell!"

(Sadly) In my despair, I remembered the blessed temple and the holy mountain of God. With seaweed and slime as my companions, I confessed my sins. I renewed my vows to the Lord, Jehovah, and prayed for deliverance.

After what I guessed were three days and three nights in this pit that felt like the bottom of the world, the fish regurgitated me on dry land. *(Sheepishly)* Apparently, the confessions of this backsliding preacher were enough to make anything sick!

When I hit the shore, not only was I willing to go to Nineveh, I wanted to go! *(Thoughtfully)* I learned a lot of things in "whale seminary." I learned that God is the Lord of all the earth. His sovereignty reaches from the depths of the ocean to the highest peak. He is Lord of all. He is the Lord God of everything and everywhere and everybody, and I wanted to proclaim it. I learned that I was not made for the dark. I was not meant to be alone.

(Excitedly) The word of the Lord came to me a second time. "Go to Nineveh!" God was giving me another chance! Although his discipline had been severe, he had not given up on me. I felt like a new man! Not only had I been washed by the sea, I had received a cleansing from God. *(With exuberance)* It was like starting all over! I had a new call, a new vision, and this time I was a volunteer. I set out immediately for Nineveh. I was no match for the wrath of God. It was good to be free. It was good to be alive!

(Animatedly) Arriving in Nineveh, I began preaching the judgment of God upon their immoral character. I told them how much God hated their sin. I denounced their pagan practices. I described the doom which hung over

their heads. To be honest with you, I enjoyed my message of judgment. I envisioned with satisfaction the destruction which a holy God would bring upon such a sinful city. After all, they were the enemy of God's chosen people. Were they not also the enemy of God?

(With a sense of wonder) As I continued to preach and harshly describe the punishment Nineveh deserved, strange things began to happen. The people began to repent. They fasted, they put on sack cloth, they sat in ashes, they humbled themselves before God. Even the king laid aside his royal attire and issued a decree for repentance throughout the city. Every man, woman and beast participated in the fast and the prayers for God's forgiveness and deliverance.

(Defensively) What I feared might happen did happen. God withheld his wrath from the people of Nineveh. Frankly, I was disappointed. After all, I had risked my life. My reputation as a prophet was at stake. I had proclaimed that in forty days the city would be destroyed. Would anybody believe me anymore? *(Angrily)* This was the word God had given me! Would God rather be compassionate than consistent? Are Ninevites more important than a Hebrew prophet's reputation?

(Wearily) I should have known this was what God would do. After all, he is merciful, slow to anger and of great kindness. I should have known I would be embarrassed, that my message of doom would not hold up. I was so humiliated! All I wanted to do was crawl off and die.

God questioned me about my anger, but I did not answer. I went outside the city, hoping that my promised destruction would come. God prepared a gourd to grow over me for shade. I was glad because I felt God was making my observation point comfortable, and I would soon see the fulfillment of the prediction.

(Pouting) **The next day the gourd died. Destruction did not come. Everything was going wrong! It was hot, very hot. I was angry, and I wanted to die. God quizzed me about my anger over the gourd. Did I have more concern for that plant than I had for people? I was confused. What was God trying to tell me?**

(Falls on his knees and prays fervently.) **Oh, God, who am I to love, and how shall I love them? Do you expect me to reflect the infinite mercy of your grace? How am I to feel about people of other races, people who do not look like me and have strange ideas?** *(Pleading)* **Teach me, Lord, to understand the scope of your love so if you ever call me again I can go without feeling angry because of your grace. Teach me to go. Oh, God, teach me to love!**

(Pauses, remaining in the prayer posture; rises slowly; quietly but firmly addresses the congregation.) **Ladies and gentlemen, I am not proud of the story which bears my name. But through those events I learned three strong lessons: one, God's love is all-inclusive; two, all people are capable of responding to God's love; three, those of us who have received his grace are under heavy obligation to share it.**

(Emphatically) **Listen! There are two places on the map of your life: the Tarshish of disobedience and the Nineveh of obedience. In which direction are you going?**

Joseph

JOSEPH, THE DREAMER
Genesis 50:14-21

We are not privy to the details of Joseph's suffering, which had to have been extensive. He is presented to us, instead, as one who, in God's power, surmounted injustice after injustice. In regard to life, Joseph seemed to have had something of a "Midas touch." No matter what awful thing befell him, something wonderful came of it. Was Joseph "charmed?" Was he a favorite of his heavenly Father, as he had been of his earthly one? No. Joseph was simply the type of person who accepted and dealt with life's blows and tried to be the best he could be in spite of them. His faith did not diminish but grew with every adversity. And it is this type of living, growing faith through which God still waits to convert tragedy into triumph for each of us.

Props: None needed
Delivery time: 20-23 minutes

(JOSEPH moves Center Stage and speaks enthusiastically to audience.) **Greetings from the patriarchs of old. I am Joseph, the son of Jacob, who was the son of Isaac, who was the son of Abraham. As you might detect, I'm proud of my heritage. Let me tell you about my family.**

My great-grandfather, Abraham, was a strong and noble patriarch. A man of obedient faith, he received a special call from God to leave the protective care of his father's tribe and travel to an unknown land on a divine assignment. The Lord God of everything promised to make him the father of a great nation. He promised to bless him and all of his descendants, if they would worship and obey.

(With a hint of confidentiality) **But there was a problem. He had no children with his wife of love, my great-grandmother, Sarah. He had a son, Ishmael, with Hagar, a handmaiden. He loved Ishmael, of course, but he desperately wanted a son by Sarah, his beloved.**

(Makes begging gestures.) **How they wanted a son and pleaded with God for one! Finally, in the fullness of time and late in life, their son was born. They named him Isaac, and he became the child of promise.**

One day, my great-grandfather's faith was severely tested when he felt God wanted him to offer his precious son, Isaac, as a human sacrifice. However, as the moment of death approached, God provided a ram in the thicket for the offering. This taught Abraham that human sacrifice would not be a requirement for worship.

Isaac, my grandfather, perhaps was less dramatic than all the other patriarchs. He married my grandmother, Rebekah, and lived a rather settled life in the Land of Promise.

Uneventful though his life may have been, he passed on his faith to his twin sons, my father, Jacob, and my uncle, Esau. They must have been a burden to my grandfather as they struggled for family prominence. There is no doubting that my father, Jacob, was clearly the winner. After all, he got the birthright and the final blessing of his father.

(Puzzled) **I often wondered why Uncle Esau would sell his right as the eldest. Why would he barter away his privilege to carry on the promise of God for a mess of pottage? Could anyone ever be that hungry?**

I wondered, too, why Grandmother Rebekah was willing to deceive her own husband and deny her eldest son in order to help my father, Jacob, receive the final blessing. Did she perceive that Jacob and not Uncle Esau was more receptive to the divine call? Was my father more committed to the concept of a chosen people? Whatever their reasons were, my father had to leave home for fear of his life once his deception was discovered.

(Slightly proud) **In many ways, my father, Jacob, was**

the most dramatic addition to the list of Hebrew patriarchs. Often, as a child, I would listen with great interest as he told the stories of his life: his dream at Bethel, where he saw the ladder reaching to heaven's gate; his years of toil for Grandfather Laban, where he worked so hard to get my mother, Rachel, and got Aunt Leah, as well; his flight from Laban's grip to be on his own with his wives, children, cattle and possessions, only to encounter his cheated brother, Esau.

What a night he must have spent before their meeting! Wrestling with his conscience, even as he struggled with the angel of God. Limping as he went along, he wondered if Uncle Esau was out for revenge, but no. It was a time of reconciliation, and my father never got over it. *(Joyfully)* It was a new day! He got a new name, "Israel." He got a new disposition! He was, indeed, God's patriarch.

You see, I do come from a rather exciting background. My family tree was heavy with the fruit of God's promise. We were a people in the making, getting ready to be a blessing to the whole world. But now, let me tell you something about me.

(Conversationally) My father had two wives, Leah and Rachel. I was the firstborn of Rachel, his favorite wife, which made me his favorite son. You may think I had it made, and at the time, I thought so too. But it's not easy being the preferred son of your father.

My brothers were filled with jealousy and hate. I made things worse by tattling on them and by sharing my adolescent dreams with our father, and this always put me in a privileged position over my brothers. They despised my attitude of superiority and well they should! *(With pain and regret)* But, oh, my dear brothers, I didn't know! I didn't know! I didn't mean to treat you like dirt. Why did my father show such partiality? He thought it was love, but for me and my brothers, it was hell.

(Pauses to recollect.) **In many ways, I had a lonely existence as a youth.** *(Pensively)* **I never will forget the day he gave me the colorful, long-sleeved coat. Such a gesture clearly set me apart from the rest of the family. I was allowed to lounge around the house in relative ease, while they worked in the fields. I could literally feel my brothers' resentment every time I wore the coat.**

(With more animation) **It was not long, however, until they had a chance to vent their bitterness on me. I was sent to their fields of labor with a word from our father. It was quite a distance from home. Seeing me approach in my special coat angered them almost beyond control.** *(Excitedly)* **At first, they wanted to kill me! They stripped me of my coat, the symbol of my arrogant pride and the object of their hate, and cast me into a pit to die. But murdering their brother was more than even their hate-filled systems could digest, so instead, they sold me to some traders on the way to Egypt.**

As I was led away, tied like a criminal to a jogging camel, I overhead my brothers saying, "Now, we are rid of that dreamer! No longer do we have to endure that household pet!"

One brother yelled to me from a distance, *(Cups hands around mouth, as if calling to someone far away)* **"Joseph! Now, do your dreaming for Egypt!"**

(Shakes head with painful memories.) **All the way to Egypt, I thought and prayed as I had never done before. Each night, I wet the sand on which I slept with my tears.** *(Falls to his knees and prays with anguish.)* **Oh, God, what is the meaning of this tragic turn of events? How can I live without my father's care? Can I ever accept what my brothers have done to me? Oh, God, these merchants are so cruel and boisterous! Their talk is vain and vulgar. Why am I the victim of such hate and scorn? Please, God, help me to endure this pain, to face the unknown. I am so**

alone, so afraid! Oh, God of my fathers, Abraham, Isaac, and Jacob, be thou my strength. Be thou my strength, for I am weak ... so weak. Amen.

(Recovers composure and resumes conversational tone.) It was a long and tiresome journey to Egypt, and at times, I thought I would perish of fatigue and thirst. However, there began to grow on me the sweet assurance that God was going to be with me. The difficulties of the desert had taught me to trust in God.

In Egypt, I became the slave of Potiphar, the captain of Pharaoh's guard. There I was, far, far away from home. A slave, when once I had been a prince; forced to work, when once I had been free from all responsibility. But God blessed my efforts, and Potiphar was so impressed that he made me overseer of his whole house.

(With slight embarrassment) My problem, however, was with his wife, who continually made advances toward me. I had been able to avoid her passionate overtures, until one day she actually caught hold of me and insisted that I lie with her. I told her I could not violate the trust of my master, her husband, and could not do this great sin against God. I tore loose from my garment and fled from her presence.

But as you know, "Hell has no fury like a woman scorned." She took my abandoned garment to her husband, Potiphar, and lied about my behavior. In fury, he had me committed to the king's prison.

At first, I reacted out of self-pity. What else could happen to me? Not only was I a foreigner and a slave, now I was a prisoner! But you know, God was with me. Even in prison, I met with some good fortune. The chief jailor put me in charge of the prisoners.

I was sensitive to the needs of the prisoners. I listened and sometimes interpreted their dreams. One in particular was a dream of Pharaoh's former butler, who was serving a prison sentence. His dream meant that he was going to be restored to Pharaoh's household. I asked him to remember me once he got out, but he didn't, and I spent two long years in prison.

(Excitedly) My big opportunity came when Pharaoh began having some dreams which troubled him. None of the wise men of Egypt could make any sense out of them. It was then the butler remembered me. He told Pharaoh of my ability to interpret his dream. From the confinement of prison, I was summoned to Pharaoh's court to hear him recall his dreams. They were about seven lean cattle eating seven fat cattle and seven thin ears of grain eating seven fat ears of grain.

In the wisdom of God, I saw his dreams as one. There would be seven years of plenty, where the fields of food would flourish. Then there would be seven years of famine with drought and disaster. With confidence that God was in control of our conversation, I proposed to Pharaoh a program of conservation for the years of plenty to see us through the years of famine.

(Slightly boastfully) He liked my idea and even made me supervisor of the project. This position was one of honor and power, second only to himself in all Egypt. I wore fine clothing, a signet ring, gold chains. Pharaoh gave me Asenath to be my wife, and I directed the storing of much food for the years of famine.

God gave me two sons. The first I named Manasseh, because God had made me forget my hardship and my father's house. The second I named Ephraim, for God had made me fruitful in the land of my affliction.

(With wonder) At times, I could hardly believe God's goodness. It was as though he had some plan for my life. As a seventeen-year-old lad, I was sold into slavery by my very own brothers. The years had brought me much pain, deception and a beautiful family and a position of

prominence and responsibility. There was only one way to explain it: God!

(Emotionally) In the second year of the famine, ten of my brothers were sent by my father, Jacob, to buy grain. It was an emotional time for me. Even though their treatment of me had been severe, I loved my brothers and longed to see my father. But I felt I must first test them to see if the years had brought any change in their dispositions.

First, I treated them like spies to test their sincerity. I left money in their sacks of grain to test their honesty. I sent for Benjamin, my youngest brother, and delayed his return to test their compassion.

In every way, I found that my brothers were repentant and humble. I could contain the truth no longer. Therefore, privately, I told them I was Joseph, their brother. I told them not to fear for what they had done to me. It was God's doing. God had turned their angry deed into a means of our survival.

"Go now," I said, "there are five more years of this famine. Bring our father, and let's live together in peace in this land of prosperity."

(Joyfully) With God's permission, Jacob came to Egypt. Oh, what a meeting we had! Years of mourning, disappointment and hurt were lost amid the joy and celebration of that moment. Seventeen happy years were spent with my father before he died. He blessed and adopted my two sons, Manasseh and Ephraim, giving them a part in his own inheritance.

After his death and according to his wishes, we carried him back to the land of Canaan to be buried with his fathers. Following our father's burial, my brothers became anxious that I might seek revenge. I assured them, however, that I forgave their transgression against me and that I would provide for them and their little ones. They were comforted when I continued to speak kindly to them.

(Quietly, intimately to audience) **Yes, I had a strange and varied life, but I learned many lessons. May I share them with you?**

In the course of life, things happen to us that do not seem favorable. My father's favoritism was not good. My brothers' hatred was hurtful. Slavery was a terrible adjustment. Lady Potiphar's accusations were demoralizing. Prison was degrading. Famine was a hardship.

But there is another truth to be considered. Nothing is totally tragic. In every circumstance there is a saving possibility. Why do I say this? Because the God we serve is not defeated by sin. He can write straight with crooked lines. He can bring good out of evil. He can bring light out of darkness. He did it for me, and he can do it for you.

If you are feeling that life has put unbearable things on you, remember there is a saving possibility in each of them.

If you are feeling resentment and bitterness toward those who have mistreated you, remember God's purpose for you is bigger than your hurt.

If you are lost in your sins and life is befuddling and confusing, then come to Jesus, because he will take care of you. Dreams do come true, but let God help you dream. And, yes, God will take care of you. *(He exits.)*

Joshua

JOSHUA, GOD'S WARRIOR
Deuteronomy 35:9; Joshua 1:1-3

Joshua's perspective is truly that of one who has "been there." He was a child of bondage who grew up to be a protégé of the leader of the exodus. He was a man whose skillful execution of divinely inspired war tactics won the Promised Land for his people. We might imagine that Joshua, who was apparently a born soldier, spent a restless forty years in the wilderness, longing to move in and claim what was promised to his people. Did he mentally map out strategies on sleepless nights? Did he study Moses intently and think about what he would do if he were in charge? Did he tremble with fear and anticipation when Moses finally ordained his leadership? However he spent his formative years, he emerged a dedicated servant who continued the tradition of being God's instrument instead of the people's idol.

Props: None needed (Costume should include easily removable shoes.)

Delivery time: 25-30 minutes

(JOSHUA enters speaking loudly and forcefully.) **"Hear this, O Israel! Fear the Lord and serve him in sincerity and truth! Put away the gods which your fathers served on the other side of the flood and in Egypt, and serve the Lord! If it seems evil for you to serve the Lord, then choose you this day whom you will serve, whether it be the gods your fathers served beyond the river or the gods of the Amorites in whose land you dwell. But as for me and my house, we will serve the Lord!"**

And the people answered and said to me: *(If there is a choir or other choral speaking group available, they can reply)* **"God forbid that we should forsake the Lord to serve other gods!"**

(Turns to and greets audience enthusiastically.) **Shalom! Shalom! Ami! Peace, peace, my people! I am Joshua, the son of Nun, and I lived during a crucial period in the**

history of Israel. My name, Joshua, means "Jehovah is salvation," and all my days, my name was a living testimony to the mighty works of God.

I am one of the few people who experienced the exodus in its entirety. For you see, my beginning goes all the way back to Egypt and the burden of its captivity. I was reared in the atmosphere of cruelty and the harsh demands of merciless taskmasters. I grew up feeling the pinch of poverty and the hopelessness that Pharaoh would always have the upper hand.

(Pauses for recollection.) I was but a young man when Moses came to Egypt, reminding us that God had heard our prayers of distress and was ready to deliver us from bondage. *(With wonder)* It was then strange and miraculous things began to happen: water turning to blood; pestilence; plagues; frogs. It was fascinating to see what God was going to do next to break a fickle Pharaoh!

(Sadly) The death of the firstborn Egyptian made a convincing impression upon him and all of us. I, too, was a firstborn saved only by the blood upon the door post of my father's house.

(Excitedly) With Pharaoh's permission, the greatest exodus of people in the history of humankind was begun with Moses as our leader. For some exciting reasons, I had the happy privilege to be his attendant.

It was as though God had given me a front row seat to all the mighty wonders he was about to perform. *(With much animation and gesturing)* The parting waters of the Red Sea were but a gateway to God's victorious future. A guiding cloud was provided. Water came up from the rock. Manna came down from heaven, and all the earth trembled as God moved his people through the wilderness.

(Thoughtfully) My first assignment was to lead the battle against Amelek. Although we were victorious, I was

little more than a spectator, as the power of God prevailed that day.

(With growing excitement) It was a soul-stirring and mind-boggling event to move with Moses into the clouds of Sinai to receive the law of the Lord. What humility! What pain! What ecstasy! What glory in that dramatic exposure to God!

(With regret) Later, however, it was a sad day at Kadesh Barnea when Israel fearfully refused to begin the conquest of the Promised Land. They listened to a cautious and negative report from those who trusted fear instead of God. Caleb and I were also a part of the surveillance team. We saw the obstacles too, but we felt with God's help we could succeed. Still, overcome by doubt, we spent many needless years wandering in a wilderness, while God's milk and honey was ready for us in the Promised Land.

(Short pause for consideration; speaks thoughtfully.) The years passed, and suddenly I found myself at the foot of Mt. Nebo hearing the charge of Moses. I was to be strong and of good courage because I would lead Israel into the land of promise. *(Incredulously)* Can you imagine what it was like to replace a man like Moses? What grace and godliness! What character of leadership and stability! I was no match for his godly skills.

Yet, Moses placed his hands upon me, and the spirit of God was with me. Therefore, the people promised to obey and follow me, even as they had harkened to Moses. It was now up to me to help God finish what Moses had begun. God assured me of his presence and power if I would be careful to do according to all the law.

I instructed the people to sanctify themselves unto God and to follow the Ark of the Covenant as a guide to where God wanted us to go. It was a strange and exciting day when we moved out to the edge of Jordan to begin the conquest of Canaan. Although I missed Moses and his saintly wisdom, the work of the Lord was unmistakable, and his power to perform was evident.

(With a sense of wonder) With the miraculous crossing of the raging Jordan, the faith of our people was greatly strengthened. It was a fascinating sight to see the wall of water wait for our passage across the dry riverbed and then return to its normal flow. Once on the other side, we erected twelve stones from the middle of the river as a memorial to the event. God's intervention at the Jordan would never be forgotten!

(Humbly) With the river behind us and the battle before us, we needed a time of preparation and worship. We renewed God's covenant with us by circumcising all the males born during our wilderness journey. We observed the Passover as a fresh reminder of God's deliverance from the bondage of Egypt.

In those days of preparation, I, too, had a special encounter with God. While contemplating the conquest of Jericho, I was confronted by a man with a drawn sword. "Are you on our side or their side?" I asked.

The man replied, "No! Neither! You are on my side, because I have come as the captain of the Lord's army!"

(Falls to knees and nearly touches forehead to floor; pauses; slips off shoes; speaks with even deeper humility.) I fell on my face and worshipped as he told me to take off my shoes, for I was on holy ground. In a unique way, God was telling me he was the captain, not I. He was in control of the conquest, not I.

In one sense, this was great assurance, but in a more profound sense, it was brokenness for me. I had to learn as leader of Israel to stand in the background so the people could see the hand of God at work. In other words, I had to fall before the walls of Jericho would fall. I was simply God's warrior with God's command, forbidden to go anywhere God did not permit.

(Rises, steps back into shoes; speaks enthusiastically, as a military man retelling his favorite war story.) **The Lord's plan for the battle of Jericho was unique. We capitalized on their fear. We had already learned from Rahab, the harlot, that the people were in great distress about the miraculous way God was leading us.**

For six days, we marched around the walls of Jericho. It was as though God was giving them further opportunity to turn from their pagan ways and appeal to the Lord Jehovah. But they did not, and on the seventh day, we marched around the city seven times. Following the seventh trip, the trumpets were blown. People shouted, and the walls tumbled down!

The conquest was swift and decisive! Nothing was left except Rahab and her family. The prevailing power of God was awesome in the victory at Jericho! *(Kneels)* **I fell on my knees in praise to Jehovah for his presence and his performance!** *(If a choir is available, here they would sing, "Battle of Jericho." JOSHUA remains kneeling throughout the song.)*

(Rises; speaks excitedly.) **What confidence and exuberance we all had as we moved to abolish the city of Ai! My reconnaissance scouts advised me that we would need only part of the army to defeat this lesser foe.** *(With embarrassment)* **But, oh, how wrong we were! What humiliation and defeat we met at Ai! The power of God had left us. "Why? Why?" I cried in earnest prayer.**

(Sadly shakes head at memory; tone is slightly accusatory.) **There was sin in the camp. For you see, God had made it clear before we entered Jericho that gold and precious things would go into the treasury of the Lord. He did not want our people lusting over the loot and fighting among themselves over the spoils of war.**

A soldier named Achan disobeyed. He took precious

things to be devoted to God and hid them in his own tent. When this sin against God was fully revealed to me, I had no choice other than to carry out the discipline of the Lord.

(With regret) In the Valley of Achor, we destroyed Achan and all that he owned. It was not an easy assignment, but a necessary one, because there is no godly conquest when sin is in the camp.

(Forcefully) Perhaps to you, capital punishment seems too severe, but at that time, it was important for Israel to learn the serious implications of violating God's will. After all, when God is the commander, it is treason to disobey his orders. Sometimes a traitor is more dangerous than the enemy.

In many ways, this Valley of Achor, the valley of judgment and discipline, was a pivotal point in our conquest of Canaan. With this cleansing and renewed commitment to the will of God, Ai was taken almost without resistance. The victory re-established our confidence in God's presence. It also created fear among all the inhabitants of Canaan.

(Enthusiastically) Surely, surely, the hand of the Lord was with us making the Gibeonites our servants! In battle with five Amorite kings, the sun stood still, and the moon refused to come up until our victory was complete. To the south, to the north, to the east and to the west, we marched as the army of the Lord from victory to victory.

Although the land was not fully conquered, my advancing years made it necessary for me to divide it among the tribes of Israel before I died. It was no small task to get everyone into an acceptable place! Some of the land had been promised by Moses. But much of the territory was divided by casting lots. A tribe had to be strong enough to hold the land it had been assigned.

(Tenderly; with admiration) A beautiful request came from Caleb, my fellow spy, who, forty-five years before at

Kadesh Barnea, agreed with me that we could take the land. He was eighty-five years old and announced he was as strong as the day he went forth as a spy. "Therefore, give me the hill country of Hebron," he said, "and I will drive out the giants in the power of God."

Needless to say, his wish was granted and his faith was rewarded. What a testimony to the strength of advancing years!

(Resumes military demeanor.) After the land allotment was completed, I summoned all the people to Shechem, where I reminded them of God's provision through the years. I strongly advised them to forsake the strange gods and serve only the Lord Jehovah. I can hear those beautiful words still echoing in my ears, "The Lord our God will we serve, and his voice we will obey."

(Pointedly to audience) Perhaps you are wondering why I have come to share those words from antiquity. I come because I am a part of your tradition. You belong to my faith. My people are your people, and my God is your God.

Now, listen to these lessons and listen well, because I have been a servant of the Lord, and I have seen too much to be silent. The Promised Land was God's idea. It was only through grace and love that my people and I were chosen to serve. Church is God's idea. In grace and love, you are called to be its servant members.

I learned to trust the Word of God as my authority, and when there was obedience, there was blessing. When there was disobedience, there was judgment. So will it be for you.

I learned the Promised Land was not entered without a struggle. The enemies of God were a formidable foe. Remember, God's victories are never cheap. But there was no joy like the joy of being in God's will in God's land!

Where are you in terms of your Promised Land? Have you begun the journey? Are you struggling for some conquest? Are you praising God for a victory?

Remember, my name Joshua means "Jehovah is salvation." I had the privilege of leading Israel into its Promised Land, but another Joshua has come. His name is Jesus, and he will lead you into the Kingdom of God. Will you hear his voice today and obey? *(He exits.)*

Judas Iscariot

JUDAS ISCARIOT
Mark 14:10-11, 17-21, 43-46

Judas' actions were indefensible, but he was a man who could easily have been a victim of his own political zeal. This infamous traitor the world loves to hate might have been naive, steadfastly single-minded and severely limited in his spiritual interpretations. That there could be any possible explanation for his savage betrayal other than purely evil intent is a new and sometimes foreign idea to many listeners. Still, when exploring the subject of Judas' motives, the question emerged: would a hate-filled, spiteful, murderous scoundrel suffer such deep remorse that he would take his own life? Maybe . . . just maybe, he was not so much sinister as he was tragically mistaken.

Props: Coins, keys and an old-looking pouch or small purse. It can have a shoulder strap or be fastened to the waist sash. It must be easily removed. Coins (especially quarters) and keys produce an audible jingling sound.

Delivery time: 20 minutes

(He strides On-Stage with an attitude that is at once defensive and defiant.) **I am Judas Iscariot, a man who gained his fame from failure and not success. I am the man you have condemned to Perdition.** *(Moves Center Stage and points accusingly at the audience.)* **You have read ugly things about me in your theology books, and history has created quite a case of contempt against me. Perhaps, you feel it is even sacrilegious for me to be here** *(Makes a sweeping, encompassing gesture)* **in your holy sanctuary. Maybe you fear I will poison the minds of the youth or upset the theology of you adults.**

(Moves closer toward the audience and implores them.) **But no, listen. You must listen to me, because if you do not hear me, you might become as I am. Oh, it is true, I betrayed the Lord for thirty pieces of silver. But I contend that I stand in the presence of many potential Judases. And**

you . . . you may become as I am, if you do not listen to me.

I do not come to you as one who condones his own behavior. I come to you as a pitiful creature, broken by the consequences of my own sin. It is out of the pit of my own misery that I speak to you. Oh, listen! Listen, as I share with you how cunningly evil worked in my life, causing me to commit the most notorious sin of the centuries. *(Quietly pleading)* Listen . . .

(Short pause; more relaxed, matter-of-fact, slightly boastful.) When I first met Jesus, I was a member of an extreme political party. Zealots, we were called. We were fanatics. We were fanatics in our loyalty and our zeal for the Jewish State. Why I, along with others, was committed to doing everything I could to embarrass Rome. We participated in assassinations, riots, insurrections, anything to rid our country of Rome — anything! Anything! Now, mind you, we were not evil men. We were men of faith, who believed that God would help us realize our dreams.

After I heard Jesus speak, after I saw his marvelous countenance and became acquainted with his personality, I realized that here was the kind of person who could lead our cause. People were calling him "Messiah," and I thought surely, surely here was the king of whom Micah spoke centuries ago. Here was Isaiah's majestic personality on whose shoulders the government would rest. Here, *here* was the kind of person with the kind of power and the kind of charm to rally an army and rid our country of Rome, once and for all. And we would be free! I saw it in his face. I heard it in his voice.

(Excitedly) Then one day, he called me — *me* — to be his disciple. I knew why they wanted me. They wanted me for my military experience. After all, we Zealots were the nearest thing there was to a Jewish army.

(Registering distaste) I didn't like some of the men he

had called. I didn't like Matthew, that curse of a tax collector, who had sold his soul to Rome. I didn't like that Simon Peter, always spouting off at the mouth. He had all the questions and all the answers.

I didn't like some of the folk that took up Jesus' time — Greeks and Gadarenes and Samaritans and Centurions. Did they not know he was a Jewish Messiah? I tried not to let this bother me much because I realized that Jesus was the kind of person who could make us great again. I put up with all of this because, after all, they had elected me treasurer of the group. That told me they wanted me to have an important place once the revolution began. So, I waited patiently for the Messiah to exert his power and to usher in his Kingdom.

(Excitedly) It all began with such greatness! There was a mood of excitement in the air. Everyone was coming to Jesus! Everyone from every country seemed to be coming to Jesus to hear him teach and to watch him as he healed the sick. I had visions of the whole world coming to him! Then we Jews would be in control and the Kingdom would come without even a battle. It was a great time to be alive! It was a great time to be a Jew!

(Boastful, almost swaggering) I listened with pride as he gave his Sermon on the Mount. Of course, I didn't understand all he was saying, but I knew he was laying the basis for his Kingdom. You know what he called us? He said, "You are the light of the world." He said, "You are the salt of the earth. You are a city set on a hill."

Oh, I was so glad . . . so glad that finally, someone recognized the greatness of us Jewish folk. *And he was the Messiah!* He was calling *us* great. He even told us to ask and we would receive; to knock, and it would be opened unto us; to seek, and we would find. Oh, surely, surely, great things were in store for us!

(Pause for concentrated recollection, then animated narrative)

One day, as he was talking to us disciples about the matters of the Kingdom, Jesus talked about the fact that he had not come to send peace but a sword. I knew then the time was about right and that any moment he was going to exert his power and usher in his Kingdom. So, I waited with delight for the Messiah to exert the power of God in some mysterious way.

Now, it still bothered me a bit that he spent so much time with the sick, the lowly, those in need. And I almost reprimanded him on one occasion for spending so much time with these needy folk, until it dawned upon me what he was doing. He was winning their allegiance. He was healing these people and gaining their admiration and their support for the cause when once the confrontation with Rome began.

Oh, it was a great beginning! Everything Jesus did seemed to be gaining momentum. Everything he said seemed to be strong and with power and meaning. The rabbis, the teachers and the religious leaders were calling *him* "Rabbi"! The disciples were calling him "Master" and "Lord." People on the streets were saying he was a prophet sent from God. Even demons were crying out and saying, "Son of God, Son of God, Son of God!"

Surely, the age of the Messiah had dawned! Surely, the great day of the Jews had arrived! And I . . . I, Judas Iscariot . . . was a part of it! It was a wonderful and an exciting time. *(Short pause; slight bewilderment)* But then strange things began to happen.

(Thoughtfully) I recall on one occasion — it was at Galilee — literally thousands had gathered on a hillside to hear him teach and to watch him heal the sick. When mealtime came, he didn't send them home to the villages to get food. You know what he did? *(With amazement)* He took two small fish and five barley loaves and fed that vast

multitude! He did! Fantastic! It was the most fascinating thing I ever saw him do.

Little huddles of people began to gather. Those who had eaten together would say among themselves, "Have you ever seen anything like that?"

Others would say, "No!"

Then someone else would say, "Let's make him our king."

Another little group huddled here would say, "What about that! Isn't it incredible? Let's make him our king!"

Another group over here had the same conversation and *(Gestures indicating Left, Center, Right)* over here and here and here, until there was one chorus chanting in unison, "Be our king! Be our king!" All over the hillside, voices were crying, "Be our king!"

(Ecstatically) Now, that was the moment I had been waiting for! And I thought he had been waiting for it also. *(Bewildered)* But you know what? He wouldn't let them. No! He wouldn't let them make him their king. He began talking about the fact that his Kingdom was not of this world. *(With impatience)* I thought, "Man, how do you ever expect to be the Messiah if you do not intend to rule this world?"

Frankly, I was disappointed. Many others were disappointed, too, and left him in wholesale numbers and followed him no more. He turned to us disciples and asked, "Will you also go away?"

And, to be honest, I almost did. But you see, I understood him better than most of those folk. I had been with him. I had shared close moments with him. I knew if there was anyone in all this world who could restore our nation to greatness, it was Jesus. So I stayed. Still, it wasn't long until I was disappointed again.

(Somewhat resigned, dejected) We were at Caesarea Philippi, and one day he began talking about going back

to Jerusalem. Can you imagine that? Going back to Jerusalem? Did he not realize the hostility and the hatred that was there, I wondered. Next, he began to talk about suffering and dying. I thought, "That's not Messiah talk! No real Messiah is supposed to suffer and die! No!"

He began talking to us about taking up our crosses and denying ourselves and following him, and, mind you, I was prepared to give my life, if need be, for the cause. But not if he was going to act so irresponsibly. Did he not know how to be a Messiah? Did he not know that Messiahs do not die? I almost left him again. "But then," I thought, "perhaps he'll change his mind. Or it might just be that he knows what he's doing."

I stayed and, of course, it was on to Jerusalem for him. He was determined to be there for Passover week. As we made our way to Jerusalem, on the outskirts of the city, in the little village of Bethany, we stopped and had a meal with Mary, Martha and Lazarus, as was often our custom. After that meal, a foolish thing happened. *(With impatience)* Mary took some very, very expensive ointment and *(Gestures indicate breaking and pouring)* broke the bottle and began to pour it upon Jesus.

I thought, "My goodness, doesn't anyone understand?" I said to Mary and those gathered there, "Don't you know that ointment could have been sold, and the money could have been used to feed the poor and the needy and all those who would be with us once the confrontation begins? Does not anybody understand?"

(Exasperated) Did not anybody realize the seriousness of our time? Everything was going wrong, it seemed. I was so disappointed. But the next day was the first day of Passover week, and as we made our entry into Jerusalem — can you believe it? — people literally lined the streets! They waved palm branches in the air and cried, "Hosanna! Hosanna to the King! God bless the

King! God bless the King of David!"

(Excitedly) Then it dawned on me: this is what Jesus had been waiting for. He did not want to be proclaimed king in Galilee. He did not want to exert his Messiahship in Caesarea Philippi. He wanted to wait for the Holy City of Jerusalem. He wanted them to proclaim him king in the City of David, the City of God.

(Boastfully) I was so proud to be a part of that little caravan following him into the city that day. I walked as close to him as I could. I wanted everyone to know that I was a friend of their king. I was one of the inner circle.

(Exasperated again, and aghast) But you won't believe what he did! With the echo of the crowd's crying, "Hosanna, Hosanna!" he marched straight into the temple and into the court of the Gentiles and in a rage and with a fury, *(Gestures indicate upturning tables, chasing, angry shouting)* he began to overturn the tables! He ran the money-changers out, shouting to them, "Don't you know my house is a house of prayer? And you have made it a den of thieves!"

Can you imagine that? Did he not know we needed that extra money coming in through the exchange of currency and through the inspection of the animals? Did he not know that we needed all the money we could get if we ever hoped to overthrow Rome?

(In disbelief) And if that was not enough, he began talking about the Pharisees, those holy men who had committed their lives to keeping all the rules and regulations of the Law, those righteous men. He called them hypocrites and other ugly names. He talked about rendering unto Caesar the things that are Caesar's. He began talking about destroying the temple and rebuilding it in three days. The temple authorities were infuriated! Did he have no sense of politics? No vision of history? Is he trying to save the world instead of us Jews? I was

embarrassed . . . I was so embarrassed! *(Looks down and shakes head.)*

(Deeply puzzled) **Did he not know how to be a Messiah? I was exasperated. I didn't know what to do. Could it be that I would have to force him to be my kind of Messiah? Would someone have to come to his rescue and force him to be the Messiah he was called of God to be?**

I knew the authorities wanted to arrest him, but they hadn't had an occasion when they could. The crowds were always around and the authorities certainly didn't want to do anything in the presence of a crowd that might cause a riot. Rome would not look kindly on a riot. But you see, I knew. I knew I could take them to a place at a time when there would be no crowds, where they could arrest Jesus without incident. So, I decided to go to the authorities. I made a deal with them. For thirty pieces of silver, *(Shakes pouch with jingling silver)* **I said, "I'll deliver your man."**

(Explains with resolve and confidence.) **Now, I had to do what I did because it was the only way I could force him to be the Messiah. I knew God wouldn't let his son die. I knew the very moment the authorities laid their hands on him, the angels would descend from heaven, my Zealot friends could come out of hiding, and all Jews could rally to the support of the cause. We could overthrow Rome and usher in the Kingdom! I knew God wasn't going to let his son die!**

(Confidence begins to slip away.) **That night, at the Passover supper, I had a strange and uneasy feeling. Every time Jesus looked at me, it seemed as though he knew exactly what I had done. Momentarily, I began to wonder, "Have I done the right thing?"**

(With bravado) **But I didn't let those thoughts preoccupy my mind very long because I knew . . . I *knew* I had done what I ought to do. I had to force his hand. I had**

to force him to exert the power of God that was within him.

Later on that night, as he talked about one betraying him, I feared the other disciples might catch on. And even if they did, I concluded that they would understand after it was all over.

Finally, he began talking about going to Gethsemane for prayer and I knew that would be the time and that would be the place. I slipped out and went to the authorities and told them I would deliver their man that night. If they would come to the Garden of Gethsemane, I would identify him with a kiss.

(Becoming restless, apprehensive) It happened as Jesus had predicted. He was there, praying quietly. When I saw the authorities coming, I eased over to Jesus and planted a kiss on his brow. When I did, I had a strange feeling that something was terribly wrong. You see, his skin was hot and damp. He was nervous and sweaty. I'd never seen him that way before. In every crisis, he had always had the utmost composure and strength and courage.

"What is happening?" I thought. Of course, I didn't have much time to be concerned about the situation because the authorities were there and they arrested him. I just stood back, expecting God's miracle to happen. But you know what? *Nothing happened.* No! Jesus let them arrest him without lifting a finger. *(Incredulously)* He even turned and rebuked Peter when he tried to fight back! *Nothing happened!* Jesus followed submissively in chains to the house of Caiaphas. Submissively, he went to the place of Pilate, to the place of Herod and back to the place of Pilate. And he never once lifted his voice in protest! Never once did he offer to fight back or to retaliate.

(Fearfully) As we walked along that night from place to place, I heard some of the soldiers talk about execution. I heard others mention something about crucifixion. Can you imagine that? Crucifixion! The process of that awkward

night continued into the early morning and I began to think, "God, when are you going to come to your son's rescue? *(More and more desperately)* What about your son? God, what about your Messiah? What about your Kingdom? God, what about us Jews? God? God, what are you going to do?"

(With deepening, intensifying regret) Apparently, God wasn't going to do anything. I came to the conclusion that God was going to let them kill his son. You should have heard the way they talked to him. They called him a blasphemer and all kinds of ugly names. They beat him, and they spit upon him, and they treated him, oh, so cruelly. Every ugly word he heard and every blow he received seemed to be coming from me.

(Voice mournful, breaking with misery and remorse) Oh, I tell you, it didn't turn out the way I wanted it to. I hadn't intended for them to treat him so unkindly. I had expected God to come to his rescue. And now, there was no God to rescue him.

(With loathing) I looked at that filthy money *(Lifts money pouch to eye level, clutches it angrily, shakes it)* — those thirty pieces of silver! I went back to the temple authorities and I threw it at their feet! *(Vehemently hurls pouch to the floor.)* I raged at them, "Men, don't you know he's innocent? Men, don't you know? He's innocent!"

One of them began to scamper around and pick up the pieces. "What will we do with this blood money?" he asked.

Blood money! Imagine that! *(Looks at hands with contempt, disgust.)* Blood money on my hands ... *blood money.* *(There is a short pause as he continues to stare at his open hands. Pitifully hopeless)* I tell you, he was innocent. He was innocent.

(Drops to the floor onto his knees, face raised in painful supplication.) Oh, my God, what have I done? What have I done? Oh, God ... what have I done? Why me? *(Buries face*

in hands.) **Why me?** *(Lifts face, weeping bitterly.)* **Oh, God, why did I have to be the one to commit the crime of the centuries? Oh, God, why me? Why did I have to be filled with such stupidity and ignorance? Oh, God, why couldn't I have understood?** *(Head drops lower and lower, voice fades, tearfully pleading.)* **Oh, God, why me? Why me? Oh, God! Why me? Why? Why . . .**

(There is a long pause while he remains kneeling, face almost touching the floor. Finally, he stands slowly, reluctantly resumes eye contact with the audience. He appears spent and greatly subdued.) **Yes, I am Judas Iscariot, a man you have condemned to Perdition. It is true I betrayed the Lord for thirty pieces of silver. But how many of you have betrayed him for less, *much* less? Unlike Peter, I never returned to the Lord to receive his mercy and forgiveness. I missed my chance to receive his grace and love. But you have a chance.** *(Points invitingly rather than accusingly.)* **Betrayers and potential Judases, you have a chance.**

(Looks down in renewed guilt and remorse.) **Oh, yes, I was a part of the force that put Jesus on a cross. Oh, yes, I participated in his excruciating pain. I helped kill Jesus. *I helped kill him.* But you know something? I have a glorious message for you. He did not stay dead. He did not *stay dead!* He arose, and he lives today! He lives that you might have a chance.** *(Triumphantly)* **He lives that you might live and live and live . . .** *(Exits celebrating.)*

Moses

Moses
Hebrews 11:23-29

From Moses, we learn about dependence on God, the importance of faith, and the dream-shattering consequences of uncontrolled anger. His reluctance to believe he was the man for God's job reminds us that our own self-assessments might not always be accurate. How often we argue with our Creator as if he really doesn't know us at all! In spite of Moses' recital of his shortcomings, God knew he would be able to deal skillfully with such leadership challenges as the fear, despondence, impatience and wavering faith of his people. God knew he could count on Moses to be a channel of his power instead of a glory-seeking hero.

If available, a tape of thunder and lightning sound effects makes a dramatic contribution to this monolog. If such a tape is not available, similar noises can be reproduced on an organ. The effort is to create an atmosphere of fear and awe.

An Off-Stage voice, deep, powerful, and commanding, will be needed for a few lines involving dialog between God and Moses.

Props: Shepherd's crook or long pole
Delivery time: 18-20 minutes

(After approximately thirty seconds of sound effects, MOSES enters, cowering and fearful of the "storm." Then sound effects stop.)

VOICE OF GOD: Moses. Moses!

MOSES: *(Frightened)* **Here I am. I . . . I'm over here.**

VOICE OF GOD: Wait! Do not come any closer! Take off your shoes. You are standing on holy ground. *(MOSES "freezes," looks around desperately, then slowly, with shaking hands, removes his shoes.)* **I am the God of Abraham, Isaac and Jacob. I have seen the affliction of my people in Egypt. I have heard their cry. I know their sufferings. I want to free them and take them to a land flowing with milk and honey. I want you to go and take my people out.**

MOSES: *(Still cowering, glancing around in near panic)*
But . . . but Lord, I'm not the one. I can't go to Egypt! I'm
a wanted man, a . . . a fugitive from justice. After all, who
would I say had sent me?

VOICE OF GOD: *I am* that *I am!* Say *I am* sent you.

MOSES: *(Gaining a little courage)* No, Lord, you've
got the wrong man. Egypt is not for me. It was long ago
and far away. I have a new home here in Midian. This is
where I belong. These are my people. Egypt will not listen
to me, and Israel will not follow me. I am a nobody, Lord.
Who listens to a nobody?

VOICE OF GOD: What is that in your hand?

MOSES: *(Looks absently at shepherd's staff he is
holding.)* Oh, this? It is just a rod, a shepherd's rod. I use
it every day with the sheep.

VOICE OF GOD: Cast it on the ground. *(MOSES
does, then jumps back in horror. If possible, produce a hissing
sound from Off-Stage.)*

MOSES: It has become a serpent!

VOICE OF GOD: Now, pick it up. *(MOSES looks in
disbelief at the "serpent" and then in the direction of God's voice.
He makes one or two fearful, halfhearted attempts to pick it up,
then finally reaches all the way down and grabs it.)* You see,
Moses, they will listen when they see the miracles I will
do through you.

MOSES: But Lord, listen to me! I am not a speaker.
My words are slow and ineffective. My voice does not
command respect.

VOICE OF GOD: Aaron, your brother, will go with
you. He will be your voice and you, Moses, will lead my
people out of bondage. Go, Moses. Go! The Spirit of the
Lord of Abraham, Isaac and Jacob is upon you. Go! Go!
Go! *(Twenty seconds of sound effects.)*

MOSES: *(Rises, slips his shoes back on and turns toward
audience.)* I went to Israel in the power of God, and Israel

was never the same. I went to Egypt in the will of God, and Egypt was never the same. I went in the fear of God, and I was never the same. I saw the power of God separate an enslaved people from their captors. I saw the miracles of God bring a proud Pharaoh to his knees. I saw the mighty God at work redeeming his people.

(Conversationally) Oh, it is true that at first, I was reluctant to accept God's assignment. I saw myself as much too small a man for such a big undertaking. God was too ambitious for me, I thought. However, I soon learned that the real issue was not my credentials, but God's design. God was much larger than my small faith. God was much more involved in this world than I ever thought possible. Listen, God may have some Egypt toward which he is leading you. If so, remember this lesson of Moses and learn it well: where the finger of God points, the hand of God will lead.

Now, let me tell you my story. It was near nightfall when Aaron and I reached Egypt. My people were returning from the brick fields. They were tired and hungry. Yet, after we told them our mission, God opened their hearts. Even though their bodies were weary with work, they rejoiced long into the night.

Our celebration was short-lived, however, for the next day, we found Pharaoh unreceptive to our mission. He had no intention of letting Israel go. This cheap labor for his pyramids was too great a prize to give up without a fight. He was furious! So great was his anger that he doubled their quotas. He made them work twice as hard. He instructed the taskmasters to keep them so busy they would have no time or energy for this God who sought their release.

(Shakes head in sad recollection.) It was a hectic time. It seemed that my presence in Egypt had done more to hurt God's people than to help them. The children of Israel

were discouraged. For them, our plan had changed from one of deliverance to one of increased oppression. Frankly, I, too, was disappointed. I began to doubt my role as a deliverer. Perhaps what I thought had been a "burning bush" in the desert was nothing more than a mirage. Perhaps what I thought was the voice of God was nothing more than my own imagination speaking out of my old dreams.

Confused and in anguish, I cried to God, *(Looks pleadingly toward God)* "Lord, what is the meaning of this? Why have you chosen to amuse yourself with this further humiliation of your people? Lord, did you call me to be a deliverer or an antagonist? Why is it not happening, Lord? Why? Why?

(With increasing desperation) It seemed everything had gone wrong. Then God commanded Aaron and me to go back to Pharaoh. He warned us that the ruler would again be unwilling but that Jehovah would use Pharaoh's reluctance to demonstrate his power for all Egypt and Israel to witness. So once again, we made our appeal. When he refused, mysterious things began to happen.

(With wonder) Somehow, the stage was set for a strange and awesome confrontation between God and Pharaoh. The water turned to blood. Frogs, gnats, flies — they came like rain. Cattle died. Plague and disease were everywhere, and still the heart of Pharaoh was unchanged. Hail and swarms of locusts destroyed the crops as total darkness prevailed for three days. Even this failed to convince the Pharaoh that God was determined to deliver his people.

One final act was needed. *(Speaks as if reluctant to talk about it.)* At first, it seemed cruel and inhuman, but it was the only language Pharaoh understood. The death angel passed through Egypt one night, and the firstborn of every Egyptian household was found dead the next morning.

As for Israel, we were instructed to kill and roast a lamb without blemish and eat it with unleavened bread and bitter herbs. We were also to sprinkle the blood upon our doorposts, and when the death angel saw the blood, he would pass over our household. We were to spend the night in readiness because God knew we would need to leave in haste the next day.

(Sadly) As Egypt awoke the next morning, sounds of weeping and misery echoed throughout the land. The awful example worked. In grief, the Pharaoh released us, ending Israel's 430-year sojourn in that land. Quickly, we made our way toward the Red Sea, only to be pursued by Pharaoh. His grief over the loss of a half-million slave workers was greater than that for the loss of his eldest son. It appeared as though our exodus would be short-lived. With the rapid approach of Pharaoh's army, we were being trapped against the Red Sea.

Some began to think this was the end, but God had other plans. As our apprehension grew, God promised that we would see the Egyptians no more. *(Incredulously, excitedly)* In an incredible miracle, the waters of the Red Sea parted, *(Gestures with hands)* and we walked across on dry land . . . on dry land! When Pharaoh's soldiers tried to follow us, they perished in the returning waters.

(Exultantly) We were safe! Safe! Egypt would bother us no more. God's deliverance at the sea greatly strengthened our morale. We were now ready to face the wilderness and the long journey to Canaan!

(Pensively) At least, I thought we were ready. Israel was a fickle people. Their faith was erratic, as their fears increased. *(With impatience)* They complained about water, and God sweetened it at Marah. They complained about food, and God provided quail and manna in the wilderness. They questioned my leadership and doubted God's desire to deliver them. Still, God fought for us against

the Amalikites at Rephidim. He led us safely to the foot of Sinai.

(*Worshipfully*) **Oh, Sinai, beautiful Sinai. Here God called me to the top of the mountain to give me the Law.** (*Gazing into the distance longingly*) **I can see it now. Oh, beautiful Sinai, thundering Sinai, smoking mountain of miracles!** (*Twenty seconds of sound effects. MOSES again cowers in awe, "shields" himself from the fearful power and majesty; falls on knees and hides face. After sound effects stop, there are five to ten seconds of silence.*)

VOICE OF GOD: **Moses, these are my laws.** (**Follow each pronouncement with approximately five seconds of sound effects.*) **I, the Lord, am your God.* You shall have no other gods before me.* You shall not make any graven images.* You shall not take the name of the Lord your God in vain.* Remember the sabbath day to keep it holy.* Honor your father and your mother.* You shall not kill.* You shall not commit adultery.* You shall not steal.* You shall not bear false witness against your neighbor.* You shall not covet.***

MOSES: (*Stands and faces audience again. With renewed confidence*) **God gave me these and other laws upon the mountain. In fact, I remained there forty days and nights receiving instructions from God. But while I was on the mountain, unfortunate things happened in the valley below. The fickle people of Israel became impatient.** (*With irritation*) **They felt I had deserted them. For a while, they lost sight of the person and the things which reminded them of God. Their faith was weak, and in their need to *see* their God, they made a golden calf.**

(*Angrily*) **This infuriated me, and in my anger, I broke the tablets of stone. I severely punished the people, but the next day, I prayed for them. I prayed that if God could not forgive them, he could also blot me out of the Book of Life.** (*With resignation*) **Even amid their rebellion and** sin, I loved my people. I pleaded to God on their behalf. He forgave their sin, and we soon moved onward toward the Promised Land.

(Conversationally) When we arrived at Kadesh, God commanded me to send spies into Canaan so we could prepare to enter. I carefully selected twelve men representing all the tribes. I asked them to look over the people, the land and the crops and to help us decide if and when we should enter.

After forty days, these men returned with a divided opinion. Ten of the spies reported that the land was fertile, and it flowed with milk and honey. But they also said there were giants in the land. The Canaanites were strong and well-fortified. Israel would be like grasshoppers before them, they said. Joshua and Caleb, however, were not as fearful. They insisted we would be able to take the land because God would be with us.

(With regret) The people listened to the majority and were overcome by fear. They wanted to overthrow me as their leader and *(With disbelief)* threatened to return to the enslavement of Egypt rather than face the awesome challenge of Canaan!

(Emphatically) I sincerely believe it was God's will for us to have entered the Promised Land from Kadesh. Yet, because of the people's lack of faith in God and in themselves, we did not go. In fact, we wandered the remainder of forty years in the wilderness until the older, faithless generation died off, and a new breed of Israelites came on the scene, ones who had the courage and stamina for conquest.

(Wearily) Once again in the wilderness, the people became impatient and complained against God and against me. All of a sudden, our camp was infested with fiery serpents which bit our people, and many died. Believing this was God's punishment, the people repented, and

again I prayed to God on their behalf. God commanded me to make a bronze serpent and to put it on a pole and lift it up high where all the people could see it. When anyone was bitten, he could look upon it and live. In this beautiful gesture of faith, we found the healing power of God.

Years passed, and the miracles of God were too numerous to count. Slowly but surely, we made our way toward Canaan. Then one day, I found myself on Mt. Nebo. From there, I could see the lovely Promised Land. *(Sadly, with resignation)* It was more beautiful than I had dreamed. But this was the end for me. Because at one point in the journey, I, too, had become a rebel, and my sin at Meribah caused me to lose God's permission to enter our blessed land. My heart was aching because I could not go to my Promised Land. *(With anguish)* I could not go!

(Hopefully) But listen, you can go! Through faith in Christ, there's a Promised Land for you. Come to him today and let him lead you to the fountain of living water, to the house of many mansions, to the land that is fairer than day.

(Begins his exit, lamenting.) I could not go! I could not go! But for you who will believe, there is a Land of Promise. *(He exits.)*

Paul

PAUL: "THE GREATEST OF THESE IS LOVE"
I Corinthians 13

The life of the apostle Paul contains such a rich variety of experiences, a single monolog can offer only a glance at the man through a glimpse of his mission. The popular "love chapter" in his letter to the Corinthians speaks so relevantly to churches today that it seems an appropriate basis for a short portrayal of one of our first missionaries. In it, he not only teaches us how to build and maintain fellowship, he reveals his depth of caring for struggling Christian congregations. This man, who began his career with passionate persecution, brought no less passion to his change of direction. He was an ardent evangelist, eager traveler, dedicated church planter, and always a living example of the love and commitment he preached.

Props: An old, small table or writing desk; parchment-colored paper

Delivery time: 20-25 minutes

_____

The following could be printed in a program or spoken by a worship leader as an introduction to the monolog:

_____

The year is A.D. 55. The great apostle Paul is in Ephesus and has just learned things are not going well in Corinth. He has been writing, but as his great heart goes out for the Corinthian church, he is moved to pray for them. Let us bow our heads and pray that God will use these moments to speak to us, even as he spoke to Corinth through Paul.

_____

(House lights are down. If available, a single spotlight On-Stage can heighten the dramatic effect. PAUL enters during audience prayer and kneels near the writing table. He speaks earnestly and with emotion.) **Oh, Lord, my heart is heavy as I come to you. My soul is weary for the people of Corinth,**

especially those of the household of faith. Corinth is such a wicked city, Lord, and there is so much temptation. The church needs you badly because it is divided. Some of the people claim to belong to me, others to Apollos, and others to Cephas.

(Slightly puzzled) I did not seek to promote myself, but rather, I sought to know nothing among them except the cross of Christ. I did not preach with eloquent words. I had no fancy sermons. I preached Christ to them, a stumbling block to the Jews and folly to the Gentiles. I fed them with the milk of your Word because they were babes. I gave them no complicated theological system which would inspire debate. But Lord, they are so divided! Why has dissension entered their ranks?

(With deep regret) There is immorality and uncleanness among them, Lord. One man is living with his father's wife, and the church has not corrected him. Help them realize their duty to keep one another clean. Teach them that their bodies are the temples of your Holy Spirit. Oh, Lord, the church of Corinth is fresh from paganism with all its immoral abuses. Give them a strong understanding of love and marriage. Cause them to see the worth of womanhood and the dignity of manhood in Christ.

(Wearily) Oh, Father, they are even confused about meat offered to idols, sold in the marketplace or served by their friends. Teach them what to eat and what not to eat. Cause them to be conscious of their influence and help them to shun all appearances of pagan worship.

(Pauses briefly to collect thoughts.) Lord, they need a better understanding of your table. Help me teach them the significance of the Lord's Supper so they may grasp the real meaning of this memorial celebration.

The problem of gifts is another thing which disturbs the church in Corinth. They compete for gifts, Lord, as though they were status symbols. Help them not to be ignorant about spiritual matters. Cause them to feel they are a part of the body of Christ, no matter what their gifts might be. Teach them love, Lord. *(Pleading)* Teach them love, love, love! Oh, Lord, please teach them love. Amen.

(He rises and moves back and forth across the stage; gestures reflect emotion and concern, as if he is praying again, silently. He suddenly becomes aware of the audience and speaks conversationally to them.) Oh, excuse me. As you have seen, I have been praying. My name is Paul, and I guess you would call me a missionary. I have been to many places with the gospel of Christ. I have started many churches. *(Earnestly)* These churches are my children in the Lord. They are my people! They have been my satisfaction and my joy, *(Sadly)* but they have also given me much heartache. You see, I have just received word from Corinth, and the news is not very good. My heart is heavy for Corinth. I have written them a long letter. *(Shakes head sadly.)* Oh, Corinth, Corinth!

Perhaps it would help me if I could tell you about Corinth. Would you be my listening ear?

(Thoughtfully) When I went to Corinth three years ago, I found a very prosperous and sinful city. A pleasure-loving city, it was a seaport with much commercial value. People were there from all over the world. What a place to share the gospel of Christ! As I began to preach, I met much opposition, especially from the Jews. They tried to get Gallio, the Roman proconsul, to do away with me, but he would have no part in this Jewish conspiracy.

It would have been easy for me to give up and leave Corinth, but the Lord spoke to me in a vision telling me not to be afraid, for he had many people in this city. Two great friends, Aquilla and Priscilla, as well as Silas and Timothy, were my constant companions. I spent eighteen months in Corinth, and a potentially strong church was forming when I left. Maybe I stayed too long.

(With regret) The news I now have is sad. The church at Corinth is having great difficulty. Evil has invaded its fellowship, and it appears that the world is gradually winning the church rather than the church winning the world.

The people are divided into at least four parties. First, there is my party, the Paul party. Many of these I led to Christ. I helped establish their church. Therefore, when disagreements arise, they base their opinion on what they assume I would say. They want their church to stay like it was when I was there.

Then, there are those who cling to Apollos. He is a gifted orator, an eloquent preacher. Many are so carried away by his articulate expressions of the gospel that he has become their authority and rallying point.

(With growing disgust) The Cephas party is a third segment of the church, and they tend to be a bit legalistic. They like Peter's strictness concerning Jewish law, and they enjoy being identified with his now-famous name.

And, of course, there is the Christ party, which suggests a subtle spiritual pride. They are the exclusivists. They think they have a corner on the truth.

As you can see, this disunity would be problem enough for the church, but there is more.

(Almost angrily) There is immorality in the church too. It is both practiced and condoned. I even heard of a young man having an affair with his stepmother! And the church did nothing about it! They have become so broadminded almost anything is allowed! They did nothing about it because they felt what a man did in private was his own business. After all, it might have been a meaningful relationship for both, they claimed.

The sin was bad enough, but when the conscience of

the church cannot be shocked by such gross immorality, evil is surely in control. The whole matter is further complicated by awkward attitudes toward marriage and women's misunderstanding of their freedom. Christian women are getting a bad reputation because decent women cover their heads in public no matter what their religion.

(With growing agitation) Listen! Things are really bad in the Corinthian church. Meat markets are full of meats left over from pagan sacrifices. Christians are confused and divided over whether or not they should eat it. The love feast, which is to be a close reproduction of the Last Supper, was designed to give the poor a good solid meal. Instead, it has become an occasion for squabbling, hurt feelings, and drunkenness. I had to forbid such eating in the church and give them strong instruction concerning the Lord's Supper.

(Sadly) Perhaps the biggest problem facing the church is the use and abuse of spiritual gifts. The Corinthians are using gifts as spiritual status symbols. The chief culprit is the gift of tongues. Somehow, they have gotten the idea that speaking in tongues makes them first-class Christians. They have lost sight of the other great gifts of the Spirit. They have forgotten that God is the giver of all gifts. They have forgotten to be content with what God has given them and to respect what he has given others.

You see what I mean? There are a lot of problems at Corinth. In my letter, I have tried to give them helpful instructions. I wish I could read you my entire letter. But since I cannot, let me share an excerpt from it. I want to speak to all their problems, especially the matter of tongues. I want to show them a more excellent way.

As you will note, most of what I have written is in the first person. I wrote this about myself. I want them to know I struggle with them. Whatever applies to them applies to me. We are in this thing together. In these four paragraphs, I have tried to offer what I feel is the only hope for the church at Corinth. Now, let me read what I believe is God's Word through me to them.

(Moves to writing desk; picks up parchment and reads.) If I speak in the tongues of men and of angels, but have not love, I am a noisy gong or a clanging cymbal. And if I have prophetic powers and understand all mysteries and all knowledge, and if I have all faith so as to remove mountains but have not love, I am nothing.

Love is patient and kind; love is not jealous nor boastful; it is not arrogant nor rude. Love does not insist on its own way; it is not irritable nor resentful. It does not rejoice at wrong, but rejoices in the right.

Love bears all things, believes all things, hopes all things, endures all things.

Love never ends. As for prophecy, it will pass away. As for tongues, they will cease. As for knowledge, it will pass away.

For our knowledge is imperfect, and our prophecy is imperfect, but when the perfect comes, the imperfect will pass away.

When I was a child, I spoke like a child, I thought like a child, I reasoned like a child. When I became a man, I gave up childish ways.

For now, we see in a mirror dimly, but then face to face. Now I know in part; then I shall understand fully, even as I have been fully understood.

So faith, hope, and love abide, these three, but the greatest of these is love.

(Returns parchment to table; speaks humbly and intimately to audience.) Thank you for listening, as I have shared the burden of my heart for Corinth. I needed to talk with someone, and you have been patient and helpful. My strong

missionary heart, however, causes me to ask, how is it with you? Where are you in your spiritual pilgrimage?

(Firmly) Where are you in relation to your church? Do you contribute to harmony and unity, or do you have a divisive spirit? Do you belong to some party or clique that rallies around a certain theological position or personality and tends to segment the body of Christ? Do you sit in the critic's corner and scorn those who struggle to serve Christ? If so, remember Corinth, and remember the only basis on which to build a church is love.

(With concern) What about your moral life? Are you committed to a life of decency in thought and action? What kind of books are you reading? What kind of movies are you seeing? What kind of deposits are you making to the memory bank of your mind? Are you developing pornographic vision? If so, remember Corinth. And remember, love is more than the free expression of emotional desire.

How do you handle other people's sin? Are you intolerant and judgmental, or do you seek to redeem and restore? Are you aware that you, too, have weaknesses of the spirit and the flesh?

Do you tolerate sin in your church? Do you choose leaders who are obstinately and openly sinful or do you select persons who, through confession, repentance and faith, are struggling to be the people of God?

Remember Corinth. They do not know how to judge nor how to restore. Only love can keep the fellowship pure.

(Moves to table and picks up letter.) Is the Holy Spirit alive in your life? Have you allowed him to cultivate your gifts? Do you feel superior because of his gifts to you, or have you retreated in inferiority, assuming that he has given you nothing? Only love, the fruit of the Holy Spirit, can blend your *(Gestures with letter toward audience)*

personality into the body of Christ.

(Begins exit, then turns back toward audience; gestures again with letter.) **Only love ...** *(He exits.)*

The Prodigal Son

THE PRODIGAL SON
Luke 15

This is a familiar story, one which has been interpreted from many perspectives. The most common point of view, however, is the narrator's or preacher's. Someone tells us *about* a young man whose life is a wonderful analogy of sinners coming home to their heavenly father. The essence of the events which brought the Prodigal home are rarely communicated. What of his dashed hopes? His shattered dreams? His failed plans? The hunger, desperation, shame, humiliation? This parable is a beacon to us not simply because it illuminates the truth that wanderers can come to their senses, but if we will look closely, it shines brightly into the dark, frightening corners of the human suffering that many experience on the long, lonely journey home.

Props: A colorful robe; a large, gold-colored ring; a pair of slip-on sandals. These should be at one end of the stage, hanging or on the floor, out of view of the audience.

Delivery time: 18-20 minutes

(*Most of this monolog is delivered as if the audience is not there. It begins with the PRODIGAL in the swine pasture distraught over his destitute condition. He holds stomach, exhibiting great pain.*) **Oh, I am hungry! I am so hungry! I have not eaten in days. My stomach is empty. My flesh cries out for food! My bones are aching with the pain of starvation.** (*Pleading*) **If only someone would give me something to eat.**

(*To a passerby*) **Hey, lady! You, there, with the basket of bread! Would you give me some to eat? Oh, please don't run away!** (*Moves as if to follow her.*) **Don't be afraid of me. I'm just hungry. I . . . I won't hurt you.**

(*To another passerby going in the other direction*) **Mister! You with the water pot! Would you give me a drink?** (*Pleading pitifully*) **Please, please do not ignore me! I'm so** thirsty. My insides are growling with the sounds of emptiness and hunger.

(Sees another passerby.) Young man! Rich young ruler with the jewels around your neck! Would you give me some money for food? They will pay me next week for keeping these pigs, but I . . . *(Ashamed but desperate)* I need something to eat now.

(Looks off into distance; speaks hopefully.) Oh, there come my friends! They'll help me. Fellows, where are you going? Into the village for some fun? *(Movements indicate they keep going and ignore him.)* Hey, wait a minute! Remember me? *(Angrily)* I'm the one who paid your gambling debts. I bought you wine before my inheritance ran out! The least you can do is bring me something to eat! Please, I can't leave these pigs. *(Looks down and around as if at pigs.)* I'm so hungry, I could eat what they're eating!

(Pauses to watch pigs; cries with desperation.) What can I do? What can I do? I am about to perish from hunger! I'm getting weaker every day. No one cares for me in this strange land. Even my former friends ignore me since my money is all gone. The swine farmer is suspicious of me, *(Haughtily)* a Jew willing to tend pigs. *(Hopelessly)* No one, absolutely no one, is going to rescue me from my plight.

(Stares off into the distance momentarily, then shakes head vigorously; speaks defensively.) No! No! I can't go home! I had enough of that when I was there. My older brother runs that show. My father never listened to me. My ideas were never any good. After all, the family business would never have been mine anyway. No matter what I did at home, I was always the younger brother!

(Forcefully) And those rules! I can't go back to all those rules. My father was such a disciplinarian. I can hear him now. "You must not run with the wrong crowd. Don't waste your money on worthless things. Don't get involved with cheap women. Don't drink strong wine for

pleasure. Remember to pray to your God because he loves you."

(With disgust) Huh! God doesn't love me, or I wouldn't be in this situation. *(Angrily)* God, if you love me, give me food! Make one of those fat cats passing by give me something to eat. God, if you really love me, get me out of this pigpen! I've never been so humiliated in all my life! *(Alternately pouts and rages.)* You don't love me, God. You are just trying to punish me because I ran away from home. You love my father and brother. All of you have a conspiracy against me! No one loves me. No one cares, especially you, God. You hate me the most! Curse you, God! Curse them all! You have brought evil upon me! I despise your very name! *(Stops suddenly and reflects with horror on what he has said. Falls to knees; speaks with deep remorse and much emotion.)*

Oh, God, what have I said? I really did not mean it! I'm so sorry. My hunger has made me crazy. I'm saying things I really do not mean. But, Lord, I'm so hungry, and I don't know what to do.

God, I have made a mess of things. I left home, and it's been downhill ever since. I have lost all my inheritance, but I've lost so much more than my money! I've lost my self-respect. Here I am like a common Gentile among the hogs. I have no pride. It's as if I am rooting around in life like these swine.

Lord, I've lost my reputation. What if the folks back home could see me now? How shocked they would be! They used to think of me as the nice, obedient younger son of my father. I can almost hear them saying, "Shame! Shame! Shame!"

Oh, God, I've lost so much. *(Timidly)* I've lost my courage, Lord. I'm becoming afraid of people and I no longer want to try. It's as though I want to wallow around in the mire of self-pity and give up. I'm losing my will to live. Oh, God, just let me die and get me out of my misery!

(With even deeper regret) **Of all things, I have lost my family. Oh, it is so lonesome out in the world without a family. I hate to admit it, Lord, but I am so homesick I could die. I'm so far away, not only in distance but in disposition. I don't belong to them anymore. My family is so good, and I am so bad.**

My father often would tell me I had great promise. He told me I would be a great success one day, if I would apply myself. Now look at me! Not only have I wasted my inheritance, I have squandered my life. I've thrown everything away, and now I am nothing. I am a nobody.

(Rises to his feet but continues imploring.) **Please, God, what can I do? I am so sorry for all the wrong things I have done and said. If only I could undo these awful months!**

Lord, I have sinned against you and all of heaven. I have put other gods before you. I have taken your name in vain. I have desecrated your holy day. I have dishonored my father and my mother. I have broken all your commandments. Please forgive me. Oh, I've hurt so many people.

(Regaining composure) **Thank you for letting me talk with you, God. I really want to be close to you, even out here in the far country. But I still don't know what to do. If only I had my inheritance money, I would take it back to my father and tell him to keep it until I was mature enough to use it wisely. But it's gone! Gone! If I had my money, I could go home as a son, but it's all gone!**

(Pauses, thinking) **If I went home, I would have to go home as a slave.** *(Another pause; with growing resolve)* **That's what I'll do! I'll go home and confess to my father how I have sinned against him and against God. I'll beg him to let me be a simple slave.** *(Excitedly)* **After all, I would rather be a slave in my father's house than king of this pigpen! At least I would have enough to eat.**

My father is a good and fair man. He will let me work my way back into his good graces. I'll work hard as a slave and maybe, just maybe, I will earn his love and respect again. If I can work in this murky mess, surely I can work harder in my father's house.

(*Moves across stage and calls into distance.*) **Oh, mister swine farmer! I'm going to leave you now. I've decided to go back to my father's house and work for him. It was nice of you to give me this job, but I was not cut out for this kind of work. And furthermore, I'm so homesick I'm about to die. I was not made for the far country. I was made for my father's house. I'm sorry, sir, but I have to go home.**

(*If appropriate, PRODIGAL could leave stage, circle around behind it and enter at other side. This could be done with quiet music playing or in lights-down silence. As PRODIGAL re-enters, he stops and looks off into the distance.*) **There's my father's house!** (*Excitedly*) **That's it, my father's house! Someone's running down the road toward me! It's . . . it's my father! He is too old to be running like that.** (*Suddenly fearful, doubtful*) **Is he running to tell me to leave, to never come in his house again?** (*With relief*) **No, wait! He is smiling! His arms are outstretched! He's not angry!**

(*Watches a moment then falls to his knees; words rush out eagerly, pleadingly.*) **Oh, Father, I have sinned against you. I should never have left. I've made a mess of things. I've lost my part of the family estate. I have shamed you and our good family name in the far country. I am no longer worthy to be your son. You have every right to disown me. I am a no-good nobody. I am nothing. Make me a slave, just your lowest slave. I'll work hard for you. I will do anything to be a part of your household again. Make me whatever you wish.**

(*Pause; looks up expectantly; listens intently, as he rises to his feet.*) **What do you mean, get up and go into the house?**

(Moves slowly toward props.) **I don't need to go in. Just give me a place in some outbuilding. I'm not worthy to go in your house. It's for family, and I have sinned away my right to be family.**

(Picks up robe.) **What's this? A robe! Surely this is not for me. This is for an honored guest! This robe is for someone special. I certainly do not deserve this robe. You want me to put it on?** *(Puts it on.)* **Oh, Father, it's beautiful. It covers these rags from the far country.**

(Picks up ring.) **A . . . a ring? Surely you are not giving me the ring! This means you are giving me back my authority. You are grafting me back into the family enterprise. But I have already wasted my part. I do not deserve any more.** *(Pensively, quietly)* **Father, there is power in this ring. Do you realize I have not handled power very well in the past?** *(Slips ring on finger. Excitedly again.)* **And shoes! Shoes are for sons! I came back just to be a slave, and slaves go barefooted.** *(With concern)* **These shoes mean I am free. I'm not sure I can handle freedom, Father. Just let me be a slave, and you make all my decisions. Then maybe I won't mess things up again.** *(Reluctantly, humbly slips on sandals. Moves across stage.)*

Is this feast for me? Father, you have killed the fatted calf! You've been saving him for a special occasion? It's true I am hungry, but just simple food would have been sufficient. You have prepared a banquet! Everyone is celebrating! *(With deep, genuine wonder)* **There is more joy over my coming home than any guest you ever had? Why? Why do you have such love for me, Father? Why are you doing all this for me when I have been such a discredit to you and my family?**

(Emphatically) **I love you, Father. I love you more than I ever thought I did. You are more than a father to me. You are my savior. You have rescued me from the famine of the far country.**

(To no one in particular) **What a celebration! I wish my
brother was here. He is probably off in the fields working.
He is such a hard worker. He would never go to the far
country and do the things I have done. He is a good
brother and good to my father.**

**It's so good to be home! There is nothing, absolutely
nothing, in the far country that compares to the joy of
being home!**

(Moves Center Stage and speaks directly to audience.) **Of
course, you know who I am. I'm the one you often call the
Prodigal Son, and what a fitting title it is. I was the most
extravagant and wasteful person you can imagine. Not only
did I waste a great portion of my father's wealth, I wasted
me. My talents, my character, my personality were being
thrown away into emptiness.**

**I left home thinking I would be free. Instead, I
became a slave, a slave to my passions, to my fears, to my
money, and to everybody from whom I could get attention.
The only freedom I found was in my father's house where
I was free to become what I was meant to be.**

**I left home to make a name for myself, a name people
would look up to and praise, especially my family. I made
a name, all right. "The prodigal," the wasted one, what
a name! The best name I have is to be the son of my father,
my family name.**

**I left home to find a pleasurable utopia, but there
is no such place. The far country promised me pleasure
but brought me pain. It offered me joy but gave me
sorrow. It vowed to give me heaven but gave me only
hell. My greatest joy is my Father's house.**

(Tenderly) **Have you been to the far country? Maybe you
are there now. Perhaps you are searching to add some zest
and meaning to your life. But I stand here to tell you, it's
not out there. There is nothing in the far country of sin
but misery and disgrace. I know . . . I have been there.**

The great God of the universe is calling you back. There is a place for you at the Father's house. There is a robe of righteousness, the ring of royalty, the shoes of salvation, and the feast of celebration.

There is a homecoming for you, and do you know why? Because there is a home. Please, oh, please, don't linger in the far country and miss the Father's embrace. *(He exits.)*

Simon Peter

SIMON PETER
John 22:15-22

Simon Peter is an excellent example of someone God used mightily in spite of some rather notable human weaknesses. Peter emerges from our New Testament pages an impulsive, talkative fellow with more than a hint of a superiority complex. Meekness and submission did not come naturally or easily to him, so we might conclude he was an unlikely companion for Jesus. Yet, Peter's faith was proclaimed the rock upon which the Christian church was to be built. What about his arrogance, his questionable loyalty when times got rough? Simon possessed an underlying strength of character which allowed him to learn a life-changing lesson from his near desertion. With the shards of his shattered self-concept, Jesus rebuilt Peter for a lifetime of commitment and unfailing trustworthiness. The expression, "strong at the broken places," is an apt description of this fascinating man.

Props: None needed

Delivery time: 15-20 minutes

(SIMON PETER swaggers On-Stage; speaks loudly and boastfully.) **I am Simon Peter! I am the roughest, toughest fisherman on the docks! I can go out farther, I can stay out longer, and I can catch more fish than anyone else. I am king of the Galilean waters! I know the sea like the back of my hand. If I can't catch any fish, then there are no fish to catch. No one, absolutely no one, out-fishes Simon Peter! My fishing business is the best in Galilee. People come from all over to do business with me because they know ol' Simon will deliver the fish.**
(Less swagger, less boastfulness) **I guess I sound pretty impressive. Perhaps you prefer to call it braggadocious. Well, that's the way I talked before Jesus came. Can you imagine me, a salty old fisherman, having anything to do with this Jesus of Nazareth? Oh, I was religious. I often**

attended the Synagogue in Capernaum and occasionally visited the Temple in Jerusalem. But my religion was the sea. I could get close to God with my nets. The smell of fish was my worship, and in the deep waters could I meditate.

(More quietly, as if remembering) But then one day, Jesus came, and it was like a breath of fresh air. He said, "Follow me and I will make you fishers of men."

Although I did not understand all the implications of his call, there was something about this Jesus that made me push fishing into the background of my life.

Isn't it strange how God calls us away from the things that seem so important to us? I never thought anyone or anything could lure me away from the water. Not only was it my livelihood, it was my way of life. Fishing met all my ego needs because I was good at it.

Jesus must have known this when he called me because he used the right words, "fishers of men." Anything that had to do with fishing appealed to me. He reached into my heart because he spoke my language.

(With wonder) Could it be that the fishing industry which had dominated so much of my time, energy and attention had strangely prepared me for discipleship? Could it be that the Messiah, this anointed one of God, could actually use the talents of one skilled only in the rudiments of fishing? I knew nothing about what following him meant, but somehow, I desperately wanted to learn.

Many times I wondered why Jesus called me. At first, *(Boastfulness easing back in)* I felt he wanted me because I was the leader of the docks. I had a way with men. I could lead his disciple band. I could whip his followers into shape! I had charisma. People listened to me. I could be his bodyguard and chief assistant.

(Not boastful; puzzled) The longer I stayed with Jesus, however, the more I realized this was not what he had in

mind. The moral and ethical demands of his teaching were quite beyond me. It did not take me long to realize that his thoughts were not my thoughts, his language was not my language, and his lifestyle was not mine. It was tantalizing! I could never attain it!

(With slight regret) My discouraging thoughts came to a climax one day while Jesus was teaching in my boat. The crowd had moved in so close to the water's edge that Jesus had to get in my boat and push off from the shore in order to address all the people. Following his lesson to which I had listened intently, Jesus suggested we move out to deep waters and cast our nets. I said, "Master, there is no need. We have fished here all night and caught nothing. The fish are not in this area."

But Jesus insisted, so I replied, "We'll do it for your sake, but don't be disappointed if nothing happens."

(Shaking head) To my utter amazement, we caught more fish than we had ever caught before! I was humiliated! Here I was, the master fisherman of Galilee, being out-fished by the master teacher! Not only was I unable to live up to his teaching, I was no match for him at the thing I did best. I had nothing to offer. I was so embarrassed and exasperated, I wanted to run and hide!

In my frustration, I fell to my knees and cried, *(With deep emotion)* "Lord, go away from me! Choose someone else because you disturb me. I cannot measure up to what you want. *(With growing desperation)* I don't belong to your way of life. I am a sinful man! I am a no-good, sinful man!"

I felt surely Jesus would give up on me and go to someone else for his leader, but he just stood there. I could see his feet firmly planted. In a few moments, he said, "Simon, don't be afraid. Don't be afraid to admit you are sinful. Don't be afraid of your weakness. Don't be afraid of your embarrassment. I have not come to taunt nor to tantalize you. I have come to heal you. I am your savior as well as your teacher. Listen, Simon, you are my kind of man. Now leave all this and follow me."

(With joy and relief) What music to my crushed and broken spirit! Humbly, yet joyfully, I left all to follow him.

It created no small rumble of talk when it was learned that Peter had forsaken his nets and followed the Nazarene. The people thought I was beside myself. But I assure you, my days with Jesus were the most productive ones of my life.

(With much enthusiasm) Can you imagine what it was like to hear him teach? "Blessed are the poor in spirit, for theirs is the Kingdom of God. Blessed are they who mourn. Blessed are the peacemakers."

On and on he went, teaching us how to repent, how to forgive, how to pray, how to trust, how to live and respect one another. He taught us the meaning of the Kingdom of God as no one else understood it.

Can you imagine what it was like to see water changed to wine? To see a blind Bartimaeus recover his sight? To see a paralytic let down through the roof and restored in body and soul? To see lepers cleansed of the cankerous disease? To see multitudes fed upon a hillside? To see boisterous waves obey his voice, and demons retreat from his presence? Surely, surely, he was the Son of God!

I never shall forget that day at Caesarea-Philippi. Jesus was sitting and wondering out loud who people thought he was. Of course, we all gave him the most popular opinions: Elijah, Jeremiah, Isaiah, John the Baptist returned from the dead. But then with a penetrating gaze, he asked, "But you . . . who do you say that I am?"

No one said anything at first. Then bursting with a faith that needed to express itself, I declared, "Why, you are the Christ, the Son of the living God! Who else?"

With a look of loving satisfaction, he said to me, "Simon, you are truly blessed because my Father has taught you this. You are a rock, and on this rock I will build my church, and the very gates of hell will not prevent its growth. I will give you the keys and your binding and loosing on earth will have eternal significance."

I didn't understand what the "keys" meant at the time, but later I did. I used those keys at Pentecost and opened the door for thousands to receive Christ. I used the keys with Cornelius, the centurion, and opened the door for Gentiles to follow Christ. I used the keys to help the infant, struggling church to gain a foothold in that pagan world.

But you see, he did not give the keys only to me, but to you also. If you belong to Christ, then you have the keys that will open the door of salvation and life for someone. Please, oh, please, use your keys because you never know when the doors you open on earth will be opened in heaven.

(With exhilaration) It was a great feeling to be honored by these words of my Lord. I was so proud of my discipleship! I felt the very God of heaven had put his stamp of approval on me. But then, Jesus began talking about going to Jerusalem, about suffering and dying. I interrupted and said, *(Emphatically)* "Stop all that talk! Hate and harm await you in Jerusalem. We won't let you suffer. We won't let you die. No! No! No!"

Jesus turned and ... and rebuked me! *(Puzzled)* He who had just called me a rock was now calling me Satan and a stumbling block! What did he mean about taking up our lives to find them again?

(With resignation) He was determined to be in Jerusalem for the Passover, and I prayed, *(Passionately)* "Oh, God, don't let him get hurt."

Our trip to Jerusalem seemed to go all right. There was a triumphant entry! Jesus survived his thrashing of the money changers when he cleansed the Temple. He taught with confidence and composure. Yet, there was apprehension in the air. We all felt something was going to happen.

That night, after the Passover meal, Jesus predicted that the time had come. Confrontation with the authorities was inevitable. He also insisted that we would all desert him. I objected. *(Boastfully again)* I was confident of my commitment. I was no fair weather friend. After all, I was a rock, remember? The others might run but not me!

(With regret) Pathetically, Jesus looked at me and said, "Simon, before the rooster crows twice — before morning has fully arrived — you will have denied me three times." Of course, I didn't believe him.

(Angrily) It was not long before soldiers came charging into Gethsemane and took him like a common criminal. I tried to fight back, but Jesus said, "No, that's not the way of my Kingdom."

I followed the soldiers who had Jesus to the courtyard of Caiaphas. Lingering in the shadows outside, I could see him standing before the high priest. In fact, I could hear most of the proceedings.

(With growing agitation) Someone built a fire, and as the flames revealed my face, a servant girl recognized me and said, "You are one of Jesus' followers." Without thinking, I said, "No, you are mistaken." But she insisted by telling everyone, "He is one of them!" Again I denied it. But others joined her, claiming that my speech gave me away. But I cursed angrily and said, "I don't know this man!"

(Remembering shock and alarm) A rooster crowed for a second time, and I remembered Jesus' words. I looked inside the door, and . . . and he was looking straight at me! *(With remorse)* Oh, Lord Jesus, I have denied you! I have! I have! I was so ashamed. I left, weeping bitterly, because I knew I had denied the best friend I ever had.

Would he ever understand? Would he ever forgive? He looked so disappointed!

(Still with shame and sadness) The ordeal of crucifixion was terrible enough within itself without the added grief of my own guilt. Oh, it hurts! It hurts so badly when you betray someone you love and didn't mean to! Oh, how I wish I could relive those moments! If I only had another chance to confess him before that courtyard crowd. I wondered, would there ever be anything else to live for?

(Greatly subdued) Of course, the resurrection was wonderful news. The excitement of God's movement was not dead. I rejoiced with everyone else in the Lord's victory over death, but deep inside, I kept wondering what he thought about me. What did he now think of his big fisherman who always had the right answers? I had been such a discredit to him in the end. If only I could have been as brave as my words. He could never again use such a weakling. So, it was back to fishing for me as I fondly remembered every moment I had spent by his side.

(With growing hopefulness) Jesus was not finished with me, however. Once again, he sought me by the water's edge. We had fished all night and caught nothing. As we were coming in, someone shouted from the shore, "Throw out the nets there."

We did and caught a net full of fish! John cried, "It is the Lord!"

(Excitedly) It was, it really was, and I jumped into the shallow water and ran to him! He had not given up on me! It was like being called all over again!

We joined him for a meal on the beach, and after we had eaten, Jesus turned to me and said, "Simon, do you love me more than these? More than nets and boats and fish?"

I said, "Yes, Lord, I love you."

Twice more he asked me, and I replied, "Oh, yes! I love you, I love you!"

He responded by asking me to care for his sheep. Three times I had denied him. Three times I had an opportunity to reaffirm my love and loyalty. *(With exhilaration and deep gratitude)* He was giving me another chance! I was forgiven! Forgiven! Oh, how I loved him! But, you know something? He loved me too! Can you imagine that? He loved me even though I had failed him. And he loves you too. Oh, how he loves us all!

He gave his life. What more can he give? Oh, how he loves you and me! The great truth is that if you will respond to his love, he will bless you beyond description. He did for me, and I saw it happen again and again. I saw him at Pentecost. I saw him with Cornelius. I saw him take a Saul of Tarsus and make an apostle of him.

(SIMON begins his exit, then turns suddenly toward audience and asks pointedly:) Do you love him? He is calling you to be fishers of men and to feed his sheep. Do you love him? Do you? *(He exits.)*

ABOUT THE AUTHOR

Dr. Calvin S. Metcalf is a native of North Carolina and holds degrees from Carson-Newman College, Jefferson City, Tennessee and Southeastern Baptist Theological Seminary in Wake Forest, North Carolina. He has served several churches in the southeast and since 1975 has been pastor of Central Baptist Church of Fountain City in Knoxville, Tennessee. An active participant in local, state and national Southern Baptist denominational life, he has chaired several boards and was president of the Tennessee Baptist Convention in 1989.

Dr. Metcalf has written and presented dramatic monologs for more than 15 years. Besides church congregations, his audiences have included Christian cruise groups, foreign mission posts, state conventions, national conferences and college classes.

His wife, Bobbie, is his costume designer-manufacturer and make-up artist. They are the parents of three grown children.

ORDER FORM

MERIWETHER PUBLISHING LTD.
P.O. BOX 7710
COLORADO SPRINGS, CO 80933
TELEPHONE: (719) 594-4422

Please send me the following books:

_____**Voices from the Bible**   **$9.95**
by Calvin S. Metcalf #CC-B173
Collection of monologs from the Old and New Testaments

_____**Scripture Plays**   **$9.95**
by Dan Neidermyer #CC-B150
A book of plays dramatizing the Holy Bible

_____**Costuming the Christmas and Easter Play**   **$6.95**
by Alice M. Staeheli #CC-B180
How to costume any religious play

_____**The Complete Banner Handbook**   **$12.95**
by Janet Litherland #CC-B172
A complete guide to banner design and construction

_____**The Official Sunday School Teachers**   **$9.95**
Handbook
by Joanne Owens #CC-B152
An indispensable aid and barrel of laughs for anyone
involved in Sunday school activities

_____**The Clown Ministry Handbook**   **$9.95**
by Janet Litherland #CC-B163
The first and most complete text on the art of clown ministry

_____**Getting Started in Drama Ministry**   **$8.95**
by Janet Litherland #CC-B154
A complete guide to Christian drama

> *I understand that I may return any book*
> *for a full refund if not satisfied.*

NAME: _____

ORGANIZATION NAME: _____

ADDRESS: _____

CITY: _____ STATE:_____ ZIP:_____

PHONE: _____

☐ **Check Enclosed**
☐ **Visa or Master Card #**_____

Signature: _____
(required for Visa/Mastercard orders)

COLORADO RESIDENTS: Please add 3% sales tax.
SHIPPING: Include $1.50 for the first book and 50¢ for each additional
book ordered.

☐ *Please send me a copy of your complete catalog of books and plays.*